One Memory at a Time

By D. G. Fulford and Bob Greene

*To Our Children's Children: Preserving Family Histories
for Generations to Come*

To Our Children's Children: Journal of Family Memories

*Notes on the Kitchen Table: Families Offer Messages
of Hope for Generations to Come*

One Memory at a Time

Inspiration and Advice
for Writing Your Family Story

D. G. FULFORD

DOUBLEDAY

New York   London   Toronto   Sydney   Auckland

PUBLISHED BY DOUBLEDAY
a division of Random House, Inc.
1540 Broadway, New York, New York 10036

DOUBLEDAY and the portrayal of an anchor with a dolphin are trademarks of
Doubleday, a division of Random House, Inc.

Book design by Paul Randall Mize

Library of Congress Cataloging-in-Publication Data
Fulford, D. G.
One memory at a time: inspiration and advice for
writing your family story / D. G. Fulford.
p. cm.
1. Genealogy—Authorship. I. Title.
CS16.F85 2000
808'.066929—dc21
00-030320
ISBN 0-385-49870-5

1 3 5 7 9 10 8 6 4 2

For Wede and the Major

Contents

FOREWORD

by Bob Greene

When my sister (the "D. G." in D. G. Fulford stands for Debby Greene) and I wrote *To Our Children's Children* in 1993, we thought we could sense the hunger for telling family histories that was beginning to form in America, but we had no idea just how strong that hunger was.

As *To Our Children's Children* continues to go back to press again and again, we now understand that the simple idea we had—people will write or record their family histories if they know what questions to ask the men and women they love—was one whose time had arrived. The book was a list of more than 1,000 questions. No one would want to answer all of them, we knew, but if families were presented with a long list of questions from which to pick and choose, this would give them the little push away from the dock that would get them started on telling their life stories. "History" is a daunting word; "genealogy" sounds dusty and dry. The 1,000-plus small, quirky questions in *To Our Children's Children* were the kinds of things families might talk about at the dinner table or at reunions. They were history with a lowercase *h*—history that did not intimidate, history that was a pleasure to recall and record.

In the years since that book was published, we have

received many notes of thanks from men and women who, using the questions as a guide, have gotten their own families' life stories down on paper or tape. They tell us they know that no book in their libraries—no book they buy in a bookstore—will ever mean as much to them as the personal histories we helped them put together for the eyes and ears of their families—the audience that means the most to them.

But they have also told us that they wished they had another tool to assist them. The questions in *To Our Children's Children* are essential to writing their family histories, they say, but they want something more: a helping hand, an empathetic coach, a voice to urge them along and assist them in getting the project completed. Questions and answers are the muscle and bones of writing a family history, they say, but they're looking for the heart and soul. They are seeking advice—both practical and spiritual—as they assemble the most important written or spoken document their family will ever own. *One Memory at a Time* is my sister's response to all of those requests—it is that helping hand for families as they put their histories together; a step-by-step guidebook to writing the histories that will make the history-writer feel he or she is not alone, that the recording of a family's story can be a joy if you have the right person beside you along the way.

Allow me some brotherly pride: My sister is the right person. No one I know understands the telling of family history better than she does; no one has a more perfect grasp of both the details and the poetry. And I think she writes beautifully.

You already want to get started on your family's history—if you didn't, you wouldn't be reading these words. Now is the time to begin. You couldn't have a better companion. Your family awaits.

One Memory at a Time

CHAPTER ONE

Overview

IN THE BEGINNING
IN THE BEGINNING THERE IS ALWAYS THE BEGINNING,
AND THIS CAN BE THE HARDEST PART.

The message of the book you hold in your hand is that family history projects have no rules. Family history projects have options. Family history is fun. It shouldn't feel like doing your taxes. You can preserve your family history in absolute freedom, just by remembering moments.

But how to begin?

Begin by planting questions in your mind. The mind loves an assignment. Your brain will take over from there. Stories start to sprout like sweet pea vines. This book is meant to lead you through the process.

· · ·

Your family history is not meant to be painted in broad brush strokes, summing up the meaning of the millennium. It is a description of your living room, of your grandmother's living room. Your life.

The original book in our series, *To Our Children's Children,* asks questions you already know the answers to. All you have to do is read them. Immediately, a story comes to mind. The book has helped hundreds of thousands of families preserve their history.

Some of those questions are interspersed throughout this book, set apart in italics. You'll see that each one can be answered in countless ways.

Your life is lived in segments. They connect decade to decade and generation to generation by an invisible thread. This thread has been handed to us by everyone who came before us.

We will be following that thread, to see where it leads.

It leads us first to that old blank page.

No one should have to face it alone.

BLANK PAGE
IT'S ONLY A PIECE OF PAPER.

The most valuable advice I've ever received wasn't from my mother.

It was from a drawing teacher. I was thirty years old at the time.

I was in an evening class, studying life drawing. Life drawing is the class in art school where students sit in a circle surrounding a nude model. They study that person and try to portray her on the page.

One would think that the model in the circle would be the most nervous person in the room. This was not the case, although I've seen some nervous ones. One poor woman flushed into a bright red rash right before my eyes.

The most nervous people in the room are the art students. They are warriors come to battle with the page. It is the most fearsome of opponents and the single most effective thing that stops a soul from starting.

The blank page stands between the artist and his or her intention.

Here's the advice, uttered by this teacher, a man I remember nothing about except these words he aimed out into the room that struck a bull's-eye with me.

"What's the worst thing that could happen?" he said

as he walked around the studio. The floor was hard and you could hear his footsteps. "What's the worst thing that could happen? Here's the worst thing that could happen: You'll waste a piece of paper."

That was the most freeing remark I ever heard.

It said, "Begin, and if you don't like it, then begin again."

It said the worst thing that could happen was not so bad at all.

It didn't say a word about the best thing.

This story has everything to do with preserving family history.

In art classes people say, "Oh, I can't draw! I can't even draw a straight line."

Of course they can't! No one can. That's why we have rulers. Drawing is a free-form art. It is not dependent upon straight lines.

Preserving family history is a free-form art, as well. Precise dates and places and researched data are available for your discovery, and they provide a strong foundation. However, facts are not all there is to a history of a family. There are treasures made of words. Stories.

Stories we may be fuzzy about until we get to thinking. Stories that we may not remember in detail, but we know how we felt at the time. Stories like the one I overheard the other day in the towel department of a store.

· · ·

A man and a woman were shopping. I heard her say she was "letting him" pick out the towels this time. Be that as it may, you don't go shopping for towels and not get into a discussion. So she was discussing her own towel preferences as he was picking up navy blues from the table and putting them back down for beiges.

"I like these," she said, standing at another table. "I like these, but I'd never buy a striped towel. I'll never have stripes. They remind me of when I was growing up and we had striped washcloths in the downstairs lavatory. They were so thin and flimsy. I guess we couldn't afford new ones. But I hated those washcloths and I told myself I'd never have striped ones again."

Her trip to the towel table ended up taking her to a much more interesting place. If she were to go home and write that thought down, her remembrance of striped washcloths past, she would have begun her family history.

Effortlessly. Naturally. Painlessly. Without even realizing she had.

One thought begets another. The striped washcloths might lead her to the realization that maybe her family didn't have enough money to make replacement washcloths a priority. She could carry the thought further. Who lived in the house with her, what did their rooms look like, what did they all eat for supper?

Family history isn't hard. We do it every day without thinking about it. Our minds naturally travel in that direction. Our minds are always going home.

Nothing lasts forever unless we write it down. When we take the time to write, we are reviewing, and reflecting back like silver mirrors.

We are asking ourselves to do something important.

Which is the place we often stop before we begin.

- Beginning is scary.
- The worst thing you can do is waste a piece of paper.
- Telling stories comes naturally.
- Nothing lasts forever unless you write it down.

LIBRARY SHELF BONES
OUR STORIES ARE ENCODED WITHIN US.
WE HAVE EASY ACCESS TO THEM.

We repeat our family stories to ourselves, subconsciously and ceaselessly. They run through our minds like blood through our veins.

Family stories are our points of reference in every situation. They are involuntary responses, like sneezing. We see a hat worn by a man on an old movie channel and our mind jumps to our grandfather; his hat, his chair, his Scottie on his lap. We roll our cart by the butcher case at the grocery store and a passing glimpse at cubes of stew beef transports us momentarily to our mother's kitchen, reaching for her blue-speckled roasting pan, the one with the lid. We remember which cupboard she kept it in, and how she would always soak it in the sink overnight to clean it.

We can be unaware of this marvelous, internal gift. It is as if our bones are library shelves, orderly and complete. The books we want are all checked in, held on reserve for us. The books that tell our stories.

I have a wonderful friend named Helen and we used to walk and talk together in the evenings, after work. Helen said this funny thing one night—this funny, obvious thing that I had never thought of.

"I'm forty-six years old," she said. "No wait. Or am I forty-seven?"

"If I'm forty-six years old," she said, settling on the lower number, "then all my organs are forty-six years old. My heart is forty-six. My eyes are forty-six."

I believe this discussion centered around us seeing ourselves as used appliances, with parts beginning to act as maddeningly as the cycle-setter on the dishwasher that you have to wriggle to get started. In this sense, though, in the family history sense, our hearts, our eyes, our ears have been walking down the road with us a long, long time.

Do you remember your first suit and tie? Your first nylons and high heels?

Our stories are on our necks and kneecaps. Do you remember the first time you tied a tie and who taught you to do so? The first time you rode a two-wheel bike and fell down in the gravel? Even muscles have memories. Your hands would recognize, in an instant, the feel of a banister familiar to you long ago. Our stories are on our cheeks; our trips to the beach before sunburn was a sin. Our stories are in our elbows; all those heavy bags we carried home from the grocery store.

One year my parents sent me a birthday card alluding to the different groups of people I had celebrated my birthday with over the years. It was they, however, and my brothers who were my constants. They had been there since birthday one, and would always be there.

You are your own constant. You and your however-many-year-old eyes and heart and scarred knee from when you were seven.

A sight, a sound, a gesture, a feeling on the skin can set an unexpected memory in motion.

By recording family history, we are doing what comes naturally. We are using memory as reference and resource. We ask ourselves the questions we know the answers to.

- We know the answers to the questions.
- A smell, a look, a gesture can bring back a memory effortlessly.
- We are our own reference and resource.

GENESIS AND GIFTS
THE GIFT OF FAMILY HISTORY IS THE MOST IMPORTANT
POSSESSION YOUR FAMILY CAN OWN.

To Our Children's Children grew from a gift. My mother and father used to spend the winter months in Florida. One year my mother took some legal pads with her. She sat in the sun writing stories, stories she remembered simply by thinking back upon her life. These were not researched documents, nor genealogy in the academic sense. They were not about who begot whom, and where and when. They were memories, stories she recalled herself or ones she remembered someone telling her.

Her grandfather came to this country alone, a fourteen-year-old boy. He slept on a counter in a relative's store in Indiana. Her mother and father added a sleeping porch to their home for muggy, Midwestern summer nights. Her father's mother was a homebody, short, round, and pleasant-looking. When our mother went to the circus as a little girl, the acrobats tossing from trapeze to trapeze scared her so much she hid her eyes and could feel her heart in her throat.

She remembered little incidents. Things that happened every day and long ago. Yet, receiving them unbidden in the mail one afternoon, I felt as if I had been given a key to a door I didn't know was there.

The next year my father surprised my brothers and me with memories he had spoken into a tape recorder. Some of these stories we had heard, most of them we hadn't. We knew the pride he felt about his military years; we didn't know that he had daydreamed about a uniformed homecoming from the time he was a boy. He even pictured the diagonal route he planned to take on this victory walk to his elementary school grounds.

He opened himself up on tape. He spoke feelings and truth. Our mother did the same on paper. The facts were there, but, more importantly, so were the feelings.

In a sense, they were introducing themselves to us.

They were expanding their definition, from parent to person. We learned about their school days, their working days, their first thoughts about each other. Their mostly ups but sometimes downs. We saw them in full spectrum, no longer just one color. And this vision, my brothers and I would agree, is the single most important one we ever hope to have.

When my brother Bob and I put together *To Our Children's Children,* its purpose was to make telling a personal history an easy thing for every family to do. We asked over one thousand specific questions. Questions that would lead to stories. Stories that would lead to other stories.

One Memory at a Time is a book of encouraging words to help you tell those stories. Sometimes you will get stuck, or feel that your stories aren't interesting enough, or that you aren't the world's best writer.

You are the best and only writer of your own story. You know the colors and you hold the crayons. This is what your family wants to hear. It is a gift only you can give them.

And, at the risk of spoiling the surprise at the end, you'll find this project to be an enormous, enlightening gift to you, the storyteller, as well.

Is there a present that sticks out in your mind? Who gave it to you? Was it a surprise, or something you'd been wanting and wanting?

When you give your stories, you are giving yourself. You are giving your parents, your grandparents, your great-grandparents to future generations. You are allowing the past and the present to shake hands with one another.

Feathered Cloche, meet your great-great-grandson, Backward Baseball Cap.

You are offering a view through a window that looks out over your lineage.

When you give your stories, you are giving pieces to a family member, pieces she never knew were missing.

- Family histories expand the definition from parent to person.
- This gift introduces the generations to each other.
- You are the only one to tell your story.

FLOOD
OUR STORIES KEEP US ALIVE.

Have you experienced a natural disaster?
An earthquake? a flood?
How was your family affected?

When I lived in Nevada, there was a flood that washed away entire lives. Whole houses and households were destroyed. Everyday life was drowned.

I spoke to a woman, an engineering professor at a university, who lost most of her possessions. All of her professorial files, containing years of research, data, knowledge, were gone. So were her clothing, her dishes, her pictures, her everything. Her biggest heartbreak, however, was the loss of her family history. Her late mother had collected anecdotes over the years; she wrote some, while family members added others. The stories grew to two hundred and fifty pages, and this engineer, with her logical bent, kept her sentimental possession in a drawer in her nightstand so it would be beside her while she slept.

Her mother had died a few years before the flood; all the aunts and uncles had passed on also. Their stories were in the nightstand, though, still a family. Ancestry on paper, ever present like a light on in the hall.

The flood took the nightstand with the rest of the possessions. The rest of the possessions the engineer could live without.

"The river could have my clothes," she said.

The loss of her mother's stories was too much to bear. She prayed. She asked for her mother's handwriting back.

"And the river gave it back," she said.

More than a month after the flood, a rancher found the nightstand drawer stuck in his barbwire fence six miles downstream. And in the drawer were the stories that her mother wrote. Her mother's handwriting, soaked and sodden, but still there.

Our stories can survive us. Our stories can survive anything. Our families live forever in our stories. Write them down.

- Stories last forever.
- Your family history will be the first thing you save when you, God forbid, escape a disaster.

STOPPERS AND HINDRANCES
ANYTHING WILL STOP YOU IF YOU LET IT.

We could spend a week discussing everything that can stop you from starting your family history project, but that would not be productive at all. Anything can stop you. These stoppers are not mere excuses. They are real. As real as today and today's errands. There is not world enough and time, you say. Or there are too many worlds and too much time. The dog ate your genealogy chart. Or there are rotten apples on your family tree.

No one is around to ask, you say. You may not consider yourself a decent writer. You may think your stories aren't interesting enough to tell, or that no one would want to listen. It's so huge, unfathomable, really. You don't know where to begin.

That's the word you're looking for. Begin. Nothing will feel better. We'll go step by step by step, every step of the way. We'll take it one memory at a time.

- Nothing feels better than finally beginning.
- This book will take you step by step.
- One memory at a time.

THINGS WE FORGOT TO REMEMBER
Everyone has stories. Not everyone is sure how to
get at them.

Once I met a man at a party who was in his sixties and
quite well read. I began talking to him about *To Our Children's Children*. He told me that he really did not recall
any family stories. He could not think of a thing, he said,
interesting enough to write down.

He told me, "You know, the only stories I ever remember hearing were those my mother told my grandmother.
My grandmother was deaf. Every Sunday, when I was a little boy, we'd go for a drive in the country. My father
would drive, and I would sit next to him, up in the front
seat. My mother and my grandmother would sit in the
backseat, and my mother would tell stories.

"My grandmother could read lips," he said, "so my
mother would speak slowly and precisely. My grandmother understood sign language, too, so my mother's
hands would talk to her in that expressive way. This was
the only chance my grandmother had to catch up with
the gossip, and the only way she could reminisce about
what Aunt Such and Such said and what ever happened
to Cousin Whoever.

"My father and I would be silent," he said. "We'd go
on these Sunday drives and we wouldn't say a word. The

whole time my mother's voice would float up to the front seat, her beautifully enunciated words painted by her hands in the back."

I said, "You don't have stories to tell?" He had reconstructed, in this conversation, the most singular of memories and brought it back to life. It was a story only he could tell.

Our minds are filing systems. Everything is in there. The merest cue can call up what we thought was lost. The things we forgot to remember.

Did you see the movie *Sleepless in Seattle?*

Tom Hanks plays a father whose wife has passed away. He subsequently falls in love with Meg Ryan, with the help of his precocious son.

But that's not the part that stayed with me. The part that stayed with me is the part that speaks directly to what we're discussing here.

There's a point in the story where the little boy, frightened and worried, admits that he's beginning to forget his mother. The father asks the boy if he remembers how she could peel an apple in one long, curly strip. The whole apple.

With that, a look came over the little boy's face. It was if his beloved, departed mother had stepped through his bedroom door one time again.

This is family history. These are the details that keep our loved ones with us. The idiosyncrasies. The peeling of apples. The Sunday drives.

I do not look at a shoe tree without thinking of my father, how he'd sit in the red and green chair by the window in the corner of my parents' bedroom. How, every day after work, he'd wipe off his business shoes with the Gold Toe ribbed sock he had just removed. Some of the socks were black, some were olive green; an Army holdover, no doubt.

I remember how he'd fit silver metal shoe trees into those big, heavy shoes—wing tips—and replace them neatly on his closet floor. Then he would slip into his loafers, sockless. He took the shoe names literally. A time for work, a time for play.

I can see the crab apple tree outside the window and his tomato plants below, in the narrow plot where the sandbox used to sit. I see my dad wearing faded madras shorts, surveying, by sight, his suburban refuge.

A silly thing—the sight of a shoe tree—brings all this back. It brings back tomatoes. It brings back the spring and the crab apple tree. It brings back the day spring turns immediately to summer.

It brings me back my father.

- We are all storytellers, whether we know it or not.
- You never know what thought or image will bring stories rushing back.

CHAPTER TWO

Family History/Family Trees

BRANCHES, TANGENTS, AND SINKS
ONE STORY LEADS TO ANOTHER, AND NOT NECESSARILY IN CHRONOLOGICAL ORDER. EXPECT TO DIGRESS. FEELINGS CAN BE AS IMPORTANT AS FACTS.

I moved into the house where I live now during a winter freeze. I find myself standing at my seventh sink, looking out my seventh kitchen window.

What do you see out your kitchen window? What kind of trees grow in your neighborhood?

I am not counting my parents' sinks; I begin counting sinks in college. So there's my college sink shared with my roommate, my single working girl sink, my newlywed sink, my new mother sink (and small wet bar where, pre-microwave, I'd warm baby bottles in hot water), my California sink, my Nevada sink, and now this, my homecoming sink back in Ohio, where I'm yet to know the trees I see out the window above it.

Having moved to this house, this sink, in winter, the trees are bare and skeletal, calligraphy against a paper sky, spelling words I don't understand. They will keep their secrets from me until spring, when they will reveal their colors in airy density, a trick only trees and clouds can do.

From my seventh sink, out my seventh kitchen window, the leafless branches make me think of the undulating arms of a belly dancer. The trees are Scheherazades, capable of telling convoluted tales in graceful ways.

Your stories will go this way and that way, too, twisting and turning.

This is fine. Permit yourself to ramble. A family history is a magnet. One thought attracts another, which, in turn, attracts another. They cling and string together. In this way, your story gets told.

It is neither science nor a rigid time line in a high school history book, where Paleolithic and Neolithic march along like soldiers. Allow—expect—tangents. Each memory grows from the fundamental center, which began as a root decades ago.

When I looked out the window above my sixth sink, in Nevada, I could see what locals called the "Hundred Mile View." To the east was a defunct mining shaft renowned for the sorry fact that it never produced enough silver ore to make an earring. I thought of it as Loser Mine. It made me sad to see it.

To the west I could see sweet Sugarloaf Mountain and the hills beyond. I could see twinkling lights from housing tracts, trailer parks, and the cars driving down Highway 50. I could see eerie, wind-driven dervishes Nevadans call dust devils that were so far away they seemed a mirage. I could catch a glimpse of the Carson River and see miles and miles of sky.

I could see so far into the distance that I didn't know what I was looking at. I only knew what I was feeling, which, of course, changed from day to day and dish to dish.

One day I discovered that this very view had been written about by a native Ohioan turned legendary Nevadan, journalist Dan De Quille.

In *History of the Big Bonanza,* which he published in 1876, he wrote: "Every artist who looks upon this weird and unsmiling landscape feels his soul stirred with a desire to paint it. No man has yet painted it—no man will ever paint it. There is that in it which no cunning in colors can reach, no skill in drawing can express. The only way in which an artist can approach the subject is by painting what he feels, not what he sees."

This is what I'm trying to get at through my tales of bare branches, tangents, and sinks: You do not need to be exacting to tell your story. You do not have to be technical, agonizing over dates and times. You can twist and turn like a tree limb in winter and write about your feelings. That is where your story lies, in the heart and its soulful ways.

A limb or a leaf? An empty shaft or silver? Great expectations, promise and loss. How did you feel at the time? And then what happened? That's the story you want to get down. You don't have to know how it will end before you begin.

- Give yourself permission to ramble.
- You can talk about feelings as well as facts.
- You don't have to know how it will end before you begin.

VANTAGE POINT / OF MICE AND MEN

YOU MAY NOT REMEMBER THINGS PRECISELY THE SAME WAY SOMEONE ELSE DOES, EVEN IF THEY WERE THERE AT THE TIME. DIFFERENT PEOPLE, DIFFERENT STORIES.

Each person's story is distinctly her own. There is the collective experience, and then there's your experience; same scene, different takes. A husband and wife working on a family history project may find themselves, for the first time in years, not speaking in the "we."

· · ·

Our mother wrote her history, our father spoke his. Their individual stories converge, then dip in and out of one another's the way dolphins swim. A brother's stories aren't the same as a sister's. Your vantage point has less to do with where you're standing than where you're coming from.

What movie affected you most in your life? Do you remember the way the movie looked mostly, or was it the story line?

When my older brother and I were children, we watched the movie *Of Mice and Men* on television. I can still remember tearing out the back door when our parents arrived home from wherever it was they had been. I wanted to tell them all about the movie. I felt I had entered the land of intellectuals, viewing such grown-up fare. It took me to depths in myself beyond Disney. I almost sputtered pouring out my description and wide-eyed review.

I told them the movie was about a dog who died. I felt as sad as Mr. Bojangles when I said it.

"It was not about a dog who died!" said my brother, who watched that same flatulent dog that I watched, get taken out to be shot like I saw, on that same black and white screen, lying on that same library floor, in that same house, right beside me.

"It was about . . ." and he gave his perfect Junior Cliff Notes version of *Of Mice and Men* right there in our drive-way. He probably spoke in footnotes.

If I were my mother, I would have given him an A.

But to me, who dreamed of dogs, who picked her desk out in her first-grade class because it was next to the wall hung with pictures of dogs, who had a china dog collection, who always played the dog when we played house, to me *Of Mice and Men* was a story about a dog who died.

Two people can experience the same thing and come away with completely different responses.

Looking back now, I can see that *Of Mice and Men* was clearly about a brown and white puppy who died. I don't even need to discuss it with my brother.

- Your story will differ from your spouse's or sibling's story.
- Each person will have his or her own response to the same situation or circumstance.

MEMORY LOSS

A MEMORY MAY BE BURIED VERY DEEP AND DIFFICULT TO FIND. YOU NEVER KNOW WHAT CAN BECOME A CONDUIT. TRY MUSIC.

But what of the ones who can't remember anymore? What of the ones, who can't remember today, much less yesterday? Why try to jog the memory of those who need

a note taped to their stove that says HOT? Why bother with
family history when you must wear a name tag to visit
your own grandmother? Why ask a question when you
don't expect an answer? What's the point? When you're
talking about a loved one's life, there always is a point.

I once saw a miracle, a miracle set to music.

The ladies were white-haired and beautiful, wearing
colorful socks and bright lipstick with fingernail polish to
match. They lived together in a home. Had this been
another time in their lives, had the clock not struck
unfairly and soon, they might have been meeting to play
mah-jongg or bridge. The clock did strike, however, for
each of these lovely ladies. Some of them had Alz-
heimer's disease, others had suffered strokes.

There was fortune, though, in their misfortune.
Once a month they got a visit from the Music Lady. She
arrived like a weekday Santa, pulling tambourines and
pompons from a glittery sack.

The ladies with memory loss oohed and ahhed like
preschoolers as each item was held up for them to see.
Age had brought them losses, but in their situation, the
loss of pretense and self-consciousness was, oddly, a gift.

The Music Lady was a troubadour on a mission. She
traveled from board-and-care home to board-and-care
home, arousing memories and brightening lives.

"'Happy days are here again,'" she sang, strumming
her guitar and smiling.

"'Enjoy yourself, it's later than you think.'"

Cheery music filled the board-and-care home. It was as if the ceiling opened up and the sun toppled down into the room. The ladies who could not remember anything else, remembered the songs that the Music Lady sang them.

"'I don't know why I love you like I do,'" they sang. "'I don't know why, I just do.'"

Somewhere in their memories, where the rest was mixed up and muddled, the lyrics to the songs survived, safe from disability and time.

The ladies danced, holding hands, as delighted to be dancing with each other as Cinderella was dancing with the Prince.

"'Baby face,'" the Music Lady sang. "'You've got the cutest little baby face.'"

"'Daisy, Daisy,'" she sang. "'Give me your answer true.'"

"Amen," said one of the ladies. It wasn't the answer, but it was true.

The ladies may not remember from month to month that the Music Lady had been there. They may not remember by the afternoon that they clapped and sang that morning. Our memories are just moments that took place once upon a time. In certain settings, only a miracle can bring them to the surface.

Do they stay there? Does it matter?

> • An unexpected memory can heal, if just for a minute.

TREE OF LIFE
STORIES ANIMATE THE FAMILY TREE.

When my daughter and I both lived out of town and would come to visit my parents, we'd sleep in one of my brother's rooms that still contains his little boy beds. My mom has enough space in her house for us to sleep separately, but we chose this room so we could spend the night together and trade magazines back and forth across the great twin bed divide.

My daughter would swap the *InStyle* she'd bought to read on the plane for my age-regressive *Mademoiselle* or *Glamour*. What those nights were really about was seizing the chance to talk to one another. We've run the gamut in topics over the years, from Barbies to boys to the birds and the bees.

I fell to pieces, weeping on her chest, the week my father died. My grown-up daughter in my grown-up brother's little boy bed. She rubbed my back and stroked my hair in a loving attempt to console the inconsolable. All the slick magazines fell to the floor. We dressed for the funeral in that room. We wore beautiful suits and dark glasses, and hardly glanced toward the mirror. We knew what we looked like. Sad.

A family tree hangs on the wall beside the bed my daughter slept in. It is a semi-elaborate work, drawn in gold and royal blue ink. It was presented to my grandmother, my Nana Amy, for her eightieth birthday, I think. It is actually more a chart than a tree, a chart consisting of squares filled in with names that diverge and connect with each other.

I've been looking at these names for years now: Adolph and Blanche, Rosa and Abraham, Morris and Anna, Frances and Allen, Eliza and Aaron, Henry and Molly, Amelia and Max. Amy and Alfred and Milfred and Ruby, Rosina, Rosa, Cora, Flora, and the poor baby girl who died at birth.

That's what they've been. Names. Names in squares, not people. This is a geometric way to look at family, reminiscent, it has always seemed to me, of the way we used to diagram sentences in school.

If Eliza and Aaron were the noun, were Alfred and Amy the verb? Was Uncle Mif the dangling participle?

This is why the stories are important. They put faces and actions and personalities to the names. They animate the squares.

My great-grandmother was Blanche. Blanche's square connects with Adolph's.

Blanche was literate and capable, according to my

mother's written history. "Not to be trifled with," she writes. "Does that sound familiar?"

Yes, it sounds familiar. It describes my mother's mother, my Nana Amy, Blanche's eldest daughter, to a T.

Blanche's son, my Nana's brother, remembers his mother as small, her features quite regular.

"She expressed her love for us in a quiet way and we regarded her highly for her assumption of both the father and mother role that became hers at a young age. Forty-six if my calculation is correct."

Adolph would have been fifty—my age—on April 13, 1914. Blanche had planned a party for him. He died on April 9, four days before his birthday.

"I remember the day he died," my great-uncle wrote in black ink on typing paper. "I was upstairs at home and I can remember my mother came in the house and said, 'It seems like a dream.'

"My mother loved picture shows and she liked the radio which came into being not too many years before her death," he wrote. "I think of my mother and father's life together as one of peace, and my mother's later life as a continuing quest for expression and knowledge."

Blanche's friends were Stella, Tillie, Hattie, Jennie and Ida, Mink, Fanny and Eliza. Eliza became my great-grandmother, too. Her son, Alfred, married Amy, my Nana.

This I know from Nana's sister, my aunt Rosina, who we called RoRo.

"By the way," RoRo wrote, "the ladies called each other 'Mrs.' for a long time after becoming friends."

A different era, a whole other time. I can see the ladies, Tillie and Stella and all the rest, arriving at a friend's porch or entry hall, wearing gloves and hats and calling out for "Mrs."

These are the things you don't get from a chart or a family tree. The images, the history lessons, the character sketches, the customs. For these, you need the memories someone has had the benevolent foresight to write down.

My daughter named one of her kittens Ruby Rosina. She swears she wasn't influenced by the blue and gold family tree. I feel, though, some of its inhabitants must have whispered to her while we slept in those twin beds, having traded magazines and stayed up talking. Mother and daughter, connected forever, through Phyllis, through Amy, through Blanche.

- Family trees and genealogy charts provide proper names, dates, and connections.
- Family histories provide stories and bring those names to life.

BUCK STOPS HERE

EVEN IF A PARENT OR GRANDPARENT IS GONE, YOU CAN
TELL WHAT YOU REMEMBER ABOUT THEM.

"No offense," my daughter said to me one day, "but I don't remember Nana that well."

Not remember Nana that well? How could she not remember Nana that well? Granted, she was only five years old when we moved across the country from Nana. But not remember Nana? That's like not remembering your own name.

Nana was my grandmother, my mother's mother. The strongest woman I ever knew. Even now, at my most assertive, I know that I'm channeling Nana.

She was beautiful and regal, like Endora on *Bewitched*. She drove a Cadillac and had a masseuse come to her home. She traveled all around the world and moved into our city's first fancy high-rise building. Her apartment was decorated in shades of powder blue and salmon, and she kept African violets and geodes on the windowsill.

She was everything a timid little girl imagines growing up to be.

Not remember Nana?

Her lamps, paintings, tables, and chairs decorate the houses of my brothers and cousins. What continuity it is to come across them. It makes me catch my breath for a minute and wonder where I am. It makes me expect her to come out from her bedroom in some silky, flowing housecoat, colorful and artfully patterned, and take my hand into hers with the beautifully painted nails.

Even when I was grown, she always held my hand.

The little table from her hallway held the favors at my niece Hannah's birthday party. One of her Parisian landscapes hangs above my cousin Kathy's hearth. My cousin Julie has the tin cookie box—she had to wrestle it away from my brother—which kept those flat raisin cookies fresh that Nana served on special occasions, like when a grandchild would come for dinner. I can taste them now as I sit typing, fifteen years after she died.

I have her makeup box and silver hand mirror and her lovely, monogrammed tea towels. For years, I wore her wedding ring. She is always with me, my Peter Pan's shadow.

Yet I did not take offense when my daughter said, "No offense." I just knew, more acutely than ever, that keeping Nana's memory alive was up to me.

The makeup box will help, and the silver mirror and tea towels, and someday my daughter will wear that ring. Until then, there are the stories.

Do you remember any special stories your grandmother or grand-father told you? Did you sit on a lap when you heard these sto-ries, or side by side on the couch, or did you hear them when you or your grandparent were walking hand-in-hand? Do you tell any of the same stories to your grandkids?

I hear regularly from people who wish their grandparent were still alive to help them with their family history project. There are so many things they'd like to ask them, so many stories they could tell.

This is true, but the buck stops here. If your grandparent has passed away, you travel down into the well of your recollection and pull up what you are able. Your memories may not be complete. There may be a whole generation of stories missing. Still, you can talk about your grandparent, both the things you remember about them, and the stories you recall them telling you about their childhood days.

When we don't have earthly access to the original source, we have legacy embedded so deeply within us that we can taste raisin cookies years later while we're typing.

Those who have gone before are the river; we are the tributaries. The river will flow on beyond our line of vision, to the point where my daughter is a Nana, and on and ever on from there.

*Did your grandmother have a favorite saying you can remember
her repeating?*

"It was not unalloyed bliss," Nana used to say when she
ran up against a circumstance that did not meet her
expectations.

Your family history project will not be unalloyed bliss.
There will be days you don't feel like working, times the
responsibility weighs too heavily on your shoulders, questions you'd like to ask a loved one who is no longer here.

Those days will pass and something like bliss will
arrive, as you write, feeling emotions you haven't felt in
years.

- Remembering is up to you.
- It is not all unalloyed bliss.

CHAPTER THREE

No Rules

SCHOOL'S OUT
THIS IS NOT A TEST. YOU ARE NOT BEING GRADED.
ERRORS CAN BE FIXED.

My mother wrote an essay about her father when she was in college. Her professor marked comments on it and gave her a grade.

The essay was entitled "Portrait of My Father." She wrote it when she was nineteen years old, a sophomore at college, one year after she lost her father, one year after she received a telephone call urging her to get home quickly and to bring a black dress.

I'm picky and protective about this primary document of my family's history. The professor's corrections jolt me and take me away from the world on the page every time I look at it.

I have reasons for mentioning this essay to you. First, I want you to remember that your words will not be graded. We all carry a teacher around in our heads, maybe not one as diligent as the professor who graded my mother's paper, but someone is always lurking there, wielding a potent red pen. When we work on our family history projects, we should not allow anyone to look over our shoulders. We should not feel that when we are finished, we need to nervously "turn it in."

We should all get gold stars simply for beginning, receive magna cum laudes for completing the project, be awarded doctorates for sitting down and putting our feelings on paper for grandchildren we may never get to know.

We should not get anxious about spelling or grammar, or chide ourselves for uninteresting adjectives. If you think something is great, it is great. If you think something is pretty, it is pretty.

I do not advocate grammatical mistakes. In fact, they make me cringe. I am a huge fan of punctuation. A misplaced apostrophe has been known to make me scream out loud, as has an innocent misspelling.

Spelling, grammar, and punctuation can always be corrected. A proofreader can be hired. A friend can give your work a quick once-over before you present it to your kin.

Spelling, grammar, and punctuation can be overlooked, as well. Overlooked and forgiven. Even treasured. Writing is talking to the page in the voice that sounds like nobody else but you.

- There is no teacher looking over your shoulder, waiting to mark you down for errors.
- Spelling, grammar, and punctuation can be fixed by an outside resource.
- Your writing is best when it sounds like you.

NO RULES
YOU CANNOT DO THIS PROJECT INCORRECTLY.

Erase the word "wrong" from your vocabulary while you are working on your family history project. While you're at it, delete "must" and "have to."

There is no right or wrong way to record your story. Each family history is as unique as the person putting it on paper. This is liberation, not a job application. These are stories, not story problems.

You are reading essay questions to which you already know the answer. It's an open book test, with your life being the open book stored on your library shelf bones. True, the answers may not spring fully formed from your head, but one sentence will follow another. Summer follows spring. Have confidence. Give yourself a chance.

There need not be a regulation beginning, middle, and end to your story. It can be a collection, a gathering of remembrances as catch-as-catch-can as a wildflower bouquet.

I recently read an account of a program that teaches grade school children to read and write by removing their fear of failure. Youngsters are encouraged to put down words the way they sound, rather than concentrating on spelling. This defrosts that frozen space between correct and incorrect. It allows children to focus on thoughts, feelings, and storytelling, rather than "*i* before *e* except after *c* and when sounding like *a*, as in 'neighbor' and 'weigh.'" "Neighbor" and "weigh" come later. Comfort and self-confidence invite them in.

We adults may find ourselves emotionally stuck in the classroom where we could have received C's and D's and forgot how to spell "kitchen." Intimidation runs deep and can last a lifetime. Throw it off. It's recess.

Preserving family history is fun, not frightening. You want to come to it thinking "oasis" rather than "chore." Consider it this way. Wouldn't you, sometimes, just sometimes, like to go out and make a household purchase without consulting *Consumer Reports*? Your family history project is based on that same sense of freedom. School's out. Sauerkraut. Teachers let the monkeys out. Put that monkey in front of a keyboard and start pounding away.

. . .

Remember this old saying? If you put enough monkeys at enough typewriters and gave them enough time, they would ultimately produce *Hamlet.*

"There is nothing either good or bad, but thinking makes it so."

—WILLIAM SHAKESPEARE, *Hamlet*

- There are no rules; no right or wrong way to do your project.
- Think freedom and fun, rather than fear and failure.
- Look at your work as an oasis instead of a chore.

MEMORIES, NOT MEDIUM
CHOOSE TO WORK IN THE MEDIUM WITH WHICH YOU ARE
MOST COMFORTABLE. THESE ARE MULTIMEDIA TIPS.

I find myself getting preoccupied with verbs. Do I say "write" your family history, "record" your family history, "type" your family history? Shall I address those of you who are working on a computer differently than typewriter typists? How about all of you writing in longhand on loose-leaf paper or those filling out the *To Our Children's Children: Journal of Family Memories*? When I say "record," am I to differentiate between "audio" and "video"?

Please know this. Any way you want to do it works. The choice of medium or method is as personal as the story. All the avenues and options are identical at the core.

I heard from a man living in the Northwest who bought a copy of *To Our Children's Children* for his mother. She had recently moved to a retirement home and he thought writing her memories down would help her pass the time.

She had difficulty getting started, so this good son got a little tricky. He bought himself a copy of the book and began casually dropping questions from it into their morning telephone calls.

"Hi, Mom. How did you sleep? What did the doctor say? *Do you remember being afraid to enter the first grade?*"

I'm sure he was a little more eloquent than that. In any case, his mother soon became an eager participant. Their phone calls grew longer, more focused. He took notes while they conversed, and entered her words into his computer after hanging up. They talked every day for six months and he learned things about her he had never known. He felt closer to her than ever. Their phone calls became something to look forward to for both, rather than the obligatory, "What time did the nurse come in?"

His mother died soon after they completed their project. He bound the work they did together and gave copies to fifteen relatives.

This end result will forever more be family treasure, but the time spent doing it—the time of really, truly talking, and not just "checking in"—is something he will cherish for the rest of his days.

Are you more comfortable speaking than writing?

If a certain medium doesn't suit you, you will not want to do your project. The method should be the last thing to stop you from enjoying one of the most satisfying endeavors you'll know.

For folks who feel more at ease speaking than writing, there is the tape recorder. For those more articulate with the written word, there's the pen and the page. The computer is an obvious choice for some, but others prefer the typewriter.

Simply said, choose the mode that comes naturally. Hunters and peckers and Bic pen scrawlers, honeyvoiced recorders and vigorous videographers, all of ye are welcome here.

My great-aunt and great-uncle's histories were both handwritten thirty years ago. Think of that. My uncle was a businessman, yet he didn't type. True, it was the era of secretaries, not administrative assistants. But an office without a typewriter or computer? What in the world did he have on his desk?

> • The medium used to tell your family history is
> entirely up to you. Some will want to tape-record,
> others will write in longhand. Some will feel com-
> fortable at a typewriter keyboard, for others only
> a computer will do. The tips and tricks and hints
> apply to everybody.
> • The memories are far more important than the
> manner and means of their compilation.

HANDWRITING

INCLUDE SOME HANDWRITING IN YOUR FAMILY HISTORY.

No medium is as personal, as immediate and telling, as
handwriting. Like a lock of hair or fingerprints, your
handwriting designates you.

What did your father's handwriting look like? Your mother's?

I asked this question in a round table group of family history writers and heard a beautiful story, one the storyteller hadn't thought about in years.

She was Asian and wrote about her wedding, forty
years before. Her father, who always struck her as an
austere and somewhat frightening man, slipped some
poems into her hand before she said her vows. They were

poems he had written, words about family life and love inscribed in his ancient, ancestral style: black ink strokes, strong, characters scrolling down the page. She had never seen this tender and emotional side of her father, but there it was, in writing, on her wedding day.

In my mother's college essay, she recalled that her father always wrote in purple ink. When she first went to college, he took her to the train. He too handed her a letter, written in that distinctive purple ink. In the letter, he expressed his great hopes for his daughter, his love and admiration. She was a capable girl, he wrote, who would grow to be a capable woman.

My mother saved that letter—in its way, a purple heart—and presented it to my daughter when she went away to college. I am sure my daughter has tucked it safely away because she too has become a capable woman. I look forward to the day when her child travels to college, reading purple words of lasting respect and approval from my mother's father long ago.

Most likely, any affectionate letter from father to daughter would be held dear no matter the format: typewritten, computer printout, or greeting card. Handwriting adds its own dimension, though. Visible personality.

I keep a grocery list my mother wrote in my jewelry box. Milk, she wrote in small, round letters. Eggs. Cheese. Cantaloupe. To me this inconsequential scrap of paper is as precious as emeralds or diamonds. It is a souvenir from my mother's every day.

I had my own handwriting analyzed once. Here is what I was told:

"In as much as you are a writer and your literary pearls must be read and understood by your audience with reasonably written letter forms, I must say that your handwriting is rather atrocious and virtually illegible.

"The letter *e* is the most used character in our alphabet. Your *e*'s resemble maybe the numeral 2. Your *y*'s are half-baked. Some of your *r*'s look like a truck smashed into them. Your *o*'s and *l*'s are OK." Thank heaven for small favors. "If you had to submit your copy in longhand, the typesetter would go berserk."

Having owned up to my shortcomings in the world of legibility, I strongly urge you to include a bit of handwriting in your family history. A paragraph, a page, or even a signature. It's a snowflake. No two are alike. Just like you. Just like your story.

- Handwriting reveals a bit of your style and flourish.
- If needs be, you can get your work transcribed for legibility.
- Use "archivally correct" materials: papers, pens, and inks. Ask for suggestions from your stationery supply store.

SENSES

**ALL OF THE SENSES ARE INVOLVED IN FAMILY HISTORY.
THE WAY THINGS SOUND, FEEL, EVEN A CHANGE IN THE
WEATHER HELPS LEAD YOU BACK.**

Family history resides in all the seasons and all the senses.
Last night was summer solstice, capping off the longest
day of the year. This must have been why I found myself
out on the deck at nine in the evening. I was reading by
nature's skylight. When the sky turned dark, all I could
do was listen.

Those trees that were bare in the wintertime, when I
first moved to my seventh sink, are lush and green now.
They are inhabited by so many birds I have to shut the
windows in the morning unless I want my awakening
thoughts to be curses at their peeping. In the summer-
time evening, though, these birds are a sensory season
ticket.

We hear our memories loud and clear. Familiar, forgotten sounds speed us back, as do sight, smell, taste, and
the feel of a soft, old blanket on your skin. I didn't realize
I'd missed seeing robins on the lawn until I returned to
Ohio. I see robins on the lawn now and understand I've
saved a place in my heart for them for twenty years.

Lightning bugs are a common memory. Tonight,
after the longest day, I saw lightning bugs above the

peony bushes and felt my father near. Once again, I opened a gift he gave me. The kind of gift you cannot touch. The gift of recognition. My dad was an aficionado of the perfect summer evening.

Around nine o'clock on summer solstice night, I hear his voice, as if he were beside me.

He asks if it is time to go "upstaice." (To those of you who do not speak Dad Greene as a Second Language, "upstaice" means upstairs.) He'd say it with a whistle at the end, and a backache groan as he rose from his chair.

"Upstaicssssse," he'd say, and he and my mother would go upstaicssssse. Nothing impeded his speech. He just thought it was funny.

I hadn't thought about "upstaice" until "upstaice" sounded in my head. In my father's voice, complete with wince and groan, and teakettle pronunciation.

We are able to go back. Sometimes a season can take us there.

Our minds are not only files, they are tape recorders, and we are all instinctive mimics. Maybe we don't do John Wayne or Humphrey Bogart, but we certainly do our parents. Only to ourselves, of course, or maybe once or twice to a brother or sister.

These are people we have listened to all of our lives. You know the voice. You know the inflection. You know the look on the face when they said what they said. I think there's a plug buried deep in our spine that connects to an outlet in the past somewhere.

If you're writing about your Aunt Violet, you will find yourself making Aunt Violet faces. And if you sit quietly and listen closely enough, you will hear Aunt Violet laugh. She had a wonderful laugh, she threw back her head and laughed skyward.

Think about the person, you'll hear the voice. Then write it down.

- Memories reside in all the senses.
- Different seasons bring back different memories.
- Think about a person and you'll hear their voice.
- We are all mimics.

AUDIOTAPE

A TAPE RECORDER CAN MAKE THE TELLING EASY AND THE LISTENING RICH.

The tape recorder is a terrific tool. You can wander around like James Bond, recording thoughts and sentences to write down later, or you can sit and tell the tape recorder your story. That's what my father did.

My dad was a frustrated actor, an entertainer in every encounter he had. Therefore, it was more fun for him to speak his story, rather than write it on paper. These tapes mean more than you can measure. I could not listen to them now, so soon after his passing, without turning into a vale of tears. However, knowing that I have them gives me certain transportation back.

My father's voice was beautiful, deep, expressive. Moist, if a voice can be described as moist. People used to tell him he sounded like the sports announcer Harry Carey, and he liked hearing that. But I never have been a sports fan, so to me, he sounded like no one else. He sounded like my father.

Except now, come to think of it, he sounded a lot like his own father. One time, when we were small, our cat Hezzleton had kittens. Dad called from work and said, "This is Grandpa." It stopped my little heart for a minute. I thought the real Grandpa Nick was calling from the great, bright blue beyond.

On his tapes, my dad spun the straw of his life into family history gold. Who knew that Rumpelstiltskin spent his youth in Akron?

How wonderful it was for me, with my ninety-minute-long commute, to stick my dad in the tape deck of my car and let his stories carry me home.

An interesting thing happened with Dad and his audiotapes that illustrates the unexpected gifts this family history project brings.

Years after he made the tapes—a fistful for me, a fistful for my brothers—he listened to them again. Probably five years had passed since he recorded them. He hadn't given them a second thought, but I was in town. I tend to bring the subject up.

So my dad sat at his desk and relistened to his life. The door to his office was partially open and I saw him as I was walking down the hall. His head was in his hands and tears were running down his cheeks. My big, strong, joking father.

Telling your stories is one thing. Hearing them told is something else again. It offers an overview, a chance to sit back and listen to all you accomplished in the span allowed. It is an opportunity to look back with pride at that person—you—who climbed over all those peaks and traversed the valleys, to shake the hand of that person—you—who lived to tell the tale. It is a chance to see yourself as a stranger would, with interest and admiration.

I think of this as that old schoolyard trick: "Ever seen a match burn twice?" The trickster lights a match, lets it flame, then blows it out. "Stick out your arm," the trickster tells you, and like a dunce, you do. The trickster lays the still hot match on your bare and trusting arm.

"Ouch!" Ha ha. The match burned twice.

I saw the match burn three times when I caught the glimpse of my dad listening to his tapes and crying.

First, he lived the life. Then he examined his experiences and recorded them for us. The match burned brightest when he became a member of his own audience. He got a chance to appreciate, like we did, every-thing he had been through and done.

For my dad, the frustrated actor, I don't think there could have been more deserved applause.

One word of warning: If you record your family history on tape, have those tapes transcribed. You don't know how well they will hold up in the future or what devices we will have on which to play them. Remember eight-tracks?

Take them to a secretarial service if you don't want to transcribe them yourself. Don't lose the stories because of inferior mechanics.

- A tape recorder can be used to catch random thoughts or to record your entire story.
- Always have your family history tapes transcribed.
- Unexpected gifts come from this project.
- Listen to your tapes years after you record them.
- Distance plus perspective equals pride.

COMPUTERS
FOR SOME, THE COMPUTER IS THE EASIEST OPTION OF ALL.

As I move through my life, from sink to sink, from type-writer to computer, I find myself at a comfortable level of need-to-know computer usage.

I use the computer the exact same way I use a three-ring notebook. I know the basics of word-processing. I only just learned how to "copy" and "paste" and I'm not even sure I have that right. Still, only knowing what I know, I know there is nothing like the computer (until the next thing). It enables one to make changes easily, thus continuing a project at a doable pace before giving up from writer's cramp or weariness from typing and retyping.

I use my computer to write and rewrite. I double-space my lines. I print pages out and scribble corrections in pencil. I fix the scribbles on the computer and print out again. I can make my way from the beginning of a thought—and delete the paltry would-be thoughts—and find myself at the end of that thought, having said what I wanted to say. What else can you ask of a machine that in my case, greets me with a happy face in the morning?

Writing your family history on the computer is a fine idea. It's easy for writing and making copies as gifts.

There are voice-powered computers, ones you can attach a video camera to, and who knows what they'll come up with in the future. There are simple devices that scan pictures onto your screen, a perfect tool for family history.

Do you and your spouse enjoy the same hobbies?
Have you taken up any new ones together, or are your individual hobbies valuable time apart for you?
As an old dog, have you learned new tricks?

I called my parents one time when I was living in California and hadn't seen them for a while. My dad answered the phone. We chatted, then I asked to speak with my mother.

"I'll have to get her," he said.

"Get her from where?" I said. I pictured those two sitting side by side in their black and white hound's-tooth checkered chairs all the time, twenty-four seven. They had been married more than fifty years. They were conjoined twins by choice and matrimony. They did everything together.

"Oh, she's back there with her new apple grinder." He put down the phone and hollered, "Phyl!"

While my dad was hollering "Phyl!" I sat at my end of the phone and wondered what he was talking about. My mother had a new apple grinder, yet she never had an old apple grinder. My mother is not the apple-grinding type. Did he mean "apple crusher"? Maybe she's eating "heart healthy" and serving him diabetic applesauce.

Suddenly my mom was on the phone, and I asked her what she'd been doing.

"Dad said you were back there with your new apple grinder," I said.

She started to laugh.

"My computer!" she said.

I remembered that, months before, my mom had bought her first computer. She had studiously learned to use it. Her instructor's name was Elvis. It was odd when she'd have computer questions and I'd have to ask, "What did Elvis say?"

The apple grinder joke was vintage Dad. In that very small phrase, in that goofy description, he was telling me just what he thought of his woman spending time with this newfangled machine.

"Daddy told me he was worried that if I ever got a computer, he'd never see me again," my mother said.

It's been known to happen. I know people who have disappeared into theirs, just got sucked in like that little girl in *Poltergeist*.

"I was trying to 'shut down' right before dinner," she said. "I don't know what I did, but everything went right off the screen. I tried not to think about it, but I worried all through dinner."

I'm sure she got some "apple grinder" comments from You Know Who, and I don't mean Elvis.

Then my mom started telling me about her friend Hope. Hope lost her husband the year before. Hope's son loaded her computer up with all kinds of games. We discussed how wonderful computers can be for seniors. We talked about how expanded the world can become, how the intellect can swell, and even about how loneliness can be somewhat dispelled. Then we hung up. We'd said many things without having to say them.

I knew my mom was, as always, efficiently making sure that her system was in place. And I knew that she, as always, would choose Dad over Elvis any day.

- A computer is terrific for adding, deleting, and correcting.
- You can make copies for your family easily on a computer.

CHAPTER FOUR

The Doing

WRITING
Have fun with it.

Working on your family history should be time you look forward to, a respite from running and responsibility. A beach chair in the sun. A place to enjoy your own company and catch your breath.

Consider it an inviting distraction, like needlepoint or a crossword puzzle. No one has you on the clock. Let your project be a destination point, a place to go, hindrance free, and immune from the stomach acid quartet of inhibition, perfectionism, resistance, and self-doubt.

Writing is conversation, talking on paper. Pretend you're on the telephone. It can be as casual as that.

But that word "history." It sounds like cumbersome duty. Purposeful writing for future generations.

Shouldn't you be wearing judicial robes and document-ing with a feather pen?

Purposeful does not mean pompous. And that word "family"? Families come in all configurations. Families are the people you are connected to and love.

The questions in *To Our Children's Children* make recording family history as easy as writing a letter or e-mail.

My brother once gave me a wonderful tip.

"Pretend you're writing a letter to Lindsey," he said. "Then take off the 'Dear Lindsey.' "

You are talking about your life and times, opening a word window to what your stint was about. You are consci-entiously creating genealogy no one will have to hunt for. It will not come to you in one fell swoop. You'll take it detail by detail. Tree by tree. You'll find the forest eventu-ally. One memory at a time.

I think we've all been a bit misled by the cartoon paint-brush that we saw on *The Wonderful World of Disney*. The image that stuck was the paintbrush which started paint-ing in one corner of the television screen, and worked its way back and forth in a speedy yet orderly fashion, leav-ing a beautiful, colorful picture in its wake.

This is not the way a painting really gets painted, nor is it how a piece of writing comes together. Writing comes together a few words at a time. Continuity and sequence are not easy to figure out, particularly in the beginning.

First, read the questions and think about them. Then collect data, notes, and memories after letting the questions steep awhile. Consolidate and cultivate your thoughts until they work their way into sentences and stories. Fruition takes place when you put your memories together in a custom pattern of your own design.

And you'll look at what you did. All those scraps of silky summer days and snippets of velvety winter ones settle into a perfectly imperfect crazy quilt. Any difficulties you encountered in the doing will up and float away.

- Family history can be as easy as writing a letter.
- You are creating genealogy no one will have to search for.
- Use your project as a welcome distraction.
- Writing is talking to the page.
- Piece by piece it comes together.

SINKS AND SEGMENTS
EVERYTHING IS MANAGEABLE WHEN YOU BREAK IT DOWN INTO SMALL ENOUGH PIECES.

I said I could write my life history by the progression of my kitchen sinks. What was I thinking about at that particular time as I stared out of that particular window. How did it ever work out? How did we get from Point A to Point B? And did the African violets bloom?

I feel I could tell my life story by word processor, as well. I bought my first typewriter as an art object at a secondhand store and tinkered with it to get it working, instead of thinking about moving to California, where I didn't want to go. It was a change for the better in my then-husband's career. I have never been fond of change. My daughter and I stayed at my parents' house while John went West and got things going. I used my mother's electric typewriter and treated myself to one of my own when I got to California in 1981. Then there was the early word processor made by Brother I referred to as the Miracle Writer, and the laptop Macintosh I bought from a salesman who kept saying, "Now you're campin'."

These memories may not mean much to you, but they bring back the specifics to me: what I was thinking and writing about all those very different times in a span of twenty years.

My life segments could be divided up into states as well: Ohio, California, Nevada, Ohio. Each state had its own segments, and sets of words to process.

Your life is a series of segments. Each segment is comprised of smaller segments. You can break them up however you wish. You can practically put brackets around them and watch how they flow from one another.

Take parenthood, for example. You were the parent of a baby. You were the parent of an eight-year-old. You were the parent of a teenager. That teenager went to college. You are the parent of an adult, who is the parent of a baby. Each of these times has its own feelings and sets of circumstances. Each time you were a slightly different you.

People often wonder about past lives, or what mysteries the afterlife promises. We overlook that we've lived many lives already, all contained in this one. You were a teenager. You were an eight-year-old. There are lots of trees in this forest and they can be seen best when looked at one by one.

What was your favorite stuffed animal?

For about six weeks or so, I found myself driving by a stuffed animal corpse on the berm of California's Ventura Freeway. It made me almost as sad as if it were someone's dead dog. Because I knew, lying right there with the long-gone stuffed animal, was some child's first knowledge that security is something you can lose.

I might be more attuned to this than most, being a huge believer in security blankets and whatever gets you through the night. Mostly I think about Tigey and my daughter. Tigey was an addendum to her, forever dangling off her hand like a frayed orange finger. He (I guess he was a he) was a fairly easy commodity to come by at the time. When one Tigey got worn to the point of extinction, I could sneakily introduce a fresh one into the system. Attrition, I guess you'd call it. I never threw a used Tigey away. One sits on the bookshelf behind me as we speak.

Tigey is more my security now than my daughter's. He reminds me of the short time in our lives when fearful moments were easy to fix.

When you get to know a child, you get to know their favorite stuffed animal. I used to get notes from my daughter's preschool teachers saying, "She's doing fine" and blah blah blah and "We like Tigey, too!" Once we hired a babysitter who did not understand the Zen of Tigey. When I went into my daughter's room, she was crying and bending over the bars of her crib, straining to reach Tigey, who had floated to the floor. As soon as he was back in her hand, she slipped into a blissful slumber. That particular babysitter never darkened our doorstep again.

This is what my daughter told me when I asked her what Tigey meant to her: "He makes me feel dreams when I'm not asleep." If that isn't peace, I don't know what is.

My daughter outgrew Tigey. She moved on to Bunny, then Barbie, then the phone and her friends. Then she went to college. Now she's driving the same freeway to work that I did when I saw the stuffed animal by the side of the road.

Were the teenage years rugged for you and your kids?

I remember a fight with my daughter. It wasn't a big fight, just a little flash fire in the car that didn't need to happen and left me feeling crummy all day.

She was fourteen. She wanted to turn up the car

radio. I didn't. We weren't even fighting over the station, which we usually did. That was what was bothering me, I think. The gap between us was getting smaller and smaller. We were entering the realm of separate but equal. I felt like our mother-daughter days were numbered and I didn't want to bicker them away.

Round one, 7:30 A.M.: She asks me for five dollars for a school play or something. I am too preoccupied to actually listen to the reason, but I hand over the money and feel magnanimous because I haven't asked her, "Don't you have money of your own?"

Round two, 7:31 A.M.: She asks me if I've picked up her graduation dress from the cleaners and dropped her film off to be developed. No, I tell her. I've been pretty busy. She tells me she's been busy, too. I know this. She's been near the breaking point with schoolwork, and I've tried to calm her by saying things like, "Who cares about the science test?" I figure this may have been poor mothering, but I sympathized with her stressful plight.

Round three, 7:33 A.M.: She asks me if she looks OK. I say yes. I ask her if I look OK. She says, "Yes, except for the shoes." She says I should pick up some white shoes for myself on Saturday, when we go shopping for her shoes to go with the graduation dress. This is the ten millionth reference to the graduation dress in three days.

Round four, 7:35 A.M.: She says, "I don't know why you have to listen to the radio so low we can't even hear it." I turn into a snarling dog. I say, "OK, you want to listen to the radio, then listen to the radio and give me back my five bucks and forget about the graduation shoes because I'm tired of your complaining!" Or words to that effect.

Knockout punch. I won.

I saw the cloud come over her face, and felt the distance between us grow. She has inherited from me a predisposition for hurt feelings. Wonderful. Hail the conquering hero. We picked up the car pool and I dropped them off at school. My daughter and I spent the day like satellites in our separate orbits with the knowledge we'd dock together at day's end.

It was no big deal, just a little fight. But in the shrinking time we had to spend together, why be at her throat like pit bull Mama? What a waste that felt like. What a crummy day.

Who did you go to your prom with? What did you wear?

At fourteen, a girl will need a dress for a dance. A dress for a dance demands alchemy from a parent—the specific and particular alchemy that spins credit card plastic into a fabulous gown.

"Park here," the girl will say after weeks of sawing at your brain stem with her fancy dress agenda. "Easy access to the Laura Ashley department."

So you will park, and you will look as she tries on dresses and sends you out for different sizes. And you will look again, and only once will you say, "It's so hot in here, I swear

I'm going to die." All the while, you will operate under the mistaken assumption that this is just another day, and just another demand from your fourteen-year-old daughter.

So you will look at your watch and tap your feet as she slips a lavender dress up and over her head—or a blue one, or a pink one.

Then you will look around the dressing room for the sorcerer because true alchemy has taken place, right there at Macy's. And you, by some accompanying grace, have been fortunate enough to watch it happen.

Your grumpy girl has been revealed to you anew. The veil of dailiness has been lifted. You see a swan, a sugar plum fairy. You see years move both forward and back. Your breath stops. You see a willowy, lovely person where a red-cheeked baby used to be.

You see a snowsuit and a Big Bird hat, your shotgun rider and constant companion, standing at the threshold of the dressing room at Macy's. In a lavender dress. Or a blue one. Or a pink one.

You stop checking your watch and tapping your feet. You try to stop thinking about the time she'll dance through the door and away.

How did you cope taking a child to college?

I was in Sedona, Arizona, on a spiritual journey in 1993. I was lying naked on my back in a stranger's home, getting a massage because there was a lot going on with me.

The masseuse asked me to define it.

"Well," I said, and started to cry. "Well, I've just dropped my daughter off at college." The tears were falling out the sides of my eyes, into my mouth where I could taste them.

I went on and on, in this nice woman's home, with her cosmic music playing. I told her how hard this was for me.

She looked me in the teary eye. "You've told me emotional," she said to me. "You haven't told me physical."

"I am all emotion," I told her. I expect everyone to know this, just by looking. I feel transparent, that everyone who sees me can see inside, like that plastic model, the Visible Woman. I wear my heart on my sleeve the way other people wear watches.

I thought that the massage lady could tell that I was twisted up in threads of separation and growth and past and future and pride and joy and sadness: Could she just knead a little and set me free?

It was a beautiful car trip to school. Scott, my beloved, drove. We went through greens and blues and fluffy white clouds, through thunderstorms and lightning. We talked and we didn't talk.

"Well," my daughter said at one weary moment, "if I'm a nerd at college, so be it."

This made me laugh so hard. It was biblical and philosophical.

The thing was, she didn't know who she'd be. She wouldn't be that same exact person who sat in that same exact school with the same exact kids since fourth grade. She would need to adjust to different ways and different weather. She would come home changed somehow. And for me, the Visible Woman, the heart on my sleeve had to start marching to a different beat.

When I walked into work the first morning after dropping my girl at college, my boss asked me if I'd lost weight.

I thought, "Ten days on the road with trail mix? I doubt it." But then I figured that what she saw was one hundred and five pounds of missing daughter. I knew you could tell by looking.

Is the house too quiet for you with the children gone? Or do you welcome the absence of commotion?

Soon after my daughter left for college, I had one of those moments. A moment so small in the grand scheme of things it could have gone by unnoticed. Once I took note of it, however, it marked a change in my life as vast as anything I'd known.

I was shutting my front door. The sun was going down, and the house was getting chilly. All was quiet: no phone, no TV, no kitchen radio. I paused long enough to hear the sounds of children playing. There were high-pitched voices and laughter coming from behind the fence out my front door.

My house was relatively hidden. I didn't know these

neighbors, yet I did recall hearing the sounds of a baby back there once. That baby must have grown big enough for playmates. I stood there and savored the sound of children playing. That's when it struck me, this defining moment. I had begun to experience children simply by sound.

It used to be that they were visuals, my own swirling mobile. For eighteen years I watched my daughter and all of her friends. I saw their clothes change through the seasons, saw them dress up for Halloween and become too cool for Halloween. I saw them in bathing suits and winter coats, and dresses for the Christmas dance.

They were always in my house, and always in my car. Their sounds were secondary to their presence. It was a constant drone, punctuated by the ringing of the phone and whatever music they were into at the given moment. I didn't really notice the noise they made. To me, it was white noise, an unnoticeable score to our life.

The presence of children is constant and overwhelming. While they are around, it doesn't seem necessary to isolate the sense they're tripping. Now my daughter was away at college. She dutifully reported what was going on by telephone.

I heard her. I did not see her.

You could argue that a child does not change much in a few months, but you would be a fool to argue that with a mother.

When my daughter would call, it would always take me a minute to recognize her voice. She sounded like a woman on the phone. My ears would grow as big as Dumbo's to hear each call's particular nuance. This was something I was getting used to and had not thought about until I heard those children playing.

We work our way through life's changes at different paces. It took me until that moment to identify this one. I had changed channels from mother in residence to mother at a distance. The children behind the fence let me know.

- Look at the segments of your life one at a time.
- Every life has its own segments. Yours won't be the same as mine.

BEGIN BY WAITING
START BY READING, NOT WRITING.

Books about writing tell you to begin by beginning; to sit yourself down and have at the page like a boxer at the sound of the bell. Put down something, anything. Make that first mark. Own that page. There are days that this works, but I also believe in waiting. I believe in keeping the lid on awhile, so the moment it is removed, stories leap out like polka-dot cloth worms from joke candy containers.

· · ·

Don't start by writing. Start by reading. Choose a section of questions and read them over. Let them percolate awhile. This is not procrastinating, it is marinating. The stories wait backstage, practicing their lines, getting better. When you take off the lid, they fly out so fast it can be startling, no matter how many times you've seen the joke, no matter how well you think you know the story. Recounting and recording is expecting everyday candy and getting circus-colored, polka-dotted, flying cloth worms instead.

- Read over the questions before you start to write.
- Your memories will surprise you.

DON'T IMAGINE YOUR AUDIENCE
DON'T LET ANYONE LOOK OVER YOUR SHOULDER, AND DON'T THINK ABOUT YOUR READERS DOWN THE LINE. WRITE FOR YOURSELF, FOR NOW.

Just as we should not look over our shoulder for an imaginary disapproving teacher, neither should we think about our audience too much. We're recording stories to last forever. We're speaking to generations to come, to our babies' babies in futuristic diapers, who, by the miracle of genetics, have our bunions and curly hair.

We cast ourselves as ancestors in deep green oil portraits. I think of myself as Good Old What's Her Name, the columnist who fell in the woods, who lived way back when.

Do not think about your descendents' descendents too much. It will keep you from writing in a natural voice. They will receive this gift of love when you get it said the way you want to say it.

This is the time for doing. Your beloveds hold reserved tickets for the best seats in the house, and for these they will patiently wait.

• Imagining your audience can make your writing self-conscious.

NONLINEAR LIVES
DO NOT WORRY ABOUT THE END RESULT WHILE YOU ARE WORKING.

We did not live our lives in a linear fashion. We went to work and raised the kids and talked on the phone while making dinner. We lived in segments made of bits and pieces. If life never felt chaotic before, this project might make it seem that way.

You know you can deal with the enormity of the family history project by breaking it down into segments. What about the expectation that, at the end, you're going to come out with a linear product?

The word "product" feels cold. It felt cold to me when I wrote it. However, you are working on this most personal of projects to have something to hold in your hand at the end. Something to read, to listen to, something that lasts forever. You might expect it to follow like a novel, with a beguiling beginning, a sensible middle, and a learn-a-lesson end. You might be thinking this should be a treatise, encyclopedic and all-encompassing, a straight line that moves the action smoothly from then to now.

That's a tall order, to be able to look back, see life, and sum it up on paper. This is daunting to think about, so some people stop, and I don't blame them. Worrying about the end result does not make it any easier to start a project.

The questions in *To Our Children's Children* are transportive. Climb aboard and record what you see out the window. The action doesn't have to pick up in the middle and be nicely resolved at the end.

If you were making a scrapbook, you might put a photograph next to a ticket with a pressed flower on the same page. Think of your project as a word scrapbook. You don't need to know how to draw a straight line to tell your story. It didn't happen that way.

- Don't be discouraged if you do not see immediately how the bits and pieces fit.
- You have not lived your life in a linear fashion, so your stories may not follow in exact sequence.
- The story will evolve; try not to worry about the final product.

NINETEEN WHATEVER

DO NOT BE OVERLY CONCERNED WITH PRECISION.
FAMILY HISTORY INVOLVES STORYTELLING RATHER THAN
THE SPECIFICITIES OF YEARS.
IT UTILIZES MEMORY MORE THAN RESEARCH.

Forget perfection. Forget it in your memory, forget it in your ability to tell the story, and forget it in the accuracy of the dates and times and participants.

Forget it because this is a difficult rabbit for the greyhound to catch. And you, being the greyhound, might choose to stop rather than endlessly follow that rabbit.

If you can't remember if it was 1943 or 1944, how much does that matter? If you can't remember if Sue was there along with Al, does that mean your story is incomplete? If the accident happened in the springtime, but for some reason you remember it as summer, does that mean you should stop there and not discuss it?

No, it doesn't. Genealogy is one thing, family history is another. Genealogy is constructing a chart, while family history is painting a picture.

Family history is enhanced by research, but it does not require it. We should immerse ourselves in the joyful act of remembering and writing our memories down.

Genealogy and family history are not mutually exclusive. You may be doing both at once, weaving hard facts and stories together. They fit perfectly, like hot fudge on French vanilla ice cream. However, some folks are not research-oriented. Or some may be like me. There is a segment on a TV show that drives me crazy. The host mentions hit songs, fads, and events that happened in a three-year span. Then the show switches to a commercial during which viewers guess the correct year.

Slap me with the history stick, but I don't really care. I just don't feel the exact year is that important. I find nothing sinful about phrases such as "I'm not sure I have this absolutely correctly . . ." or "I remember something about . . ."

I remember "Up on the Roof" by the Drifters, and how Lindsey used to call and tell me to quick turn on my turquoise blue radio. I'd stick my head out my bedroom window and breathe fresh air with the Drifters singing.

Was it spring air or was it summer air? It was winter air, decades later, when the pianist, at my request, played "Up on the Roof" at the funeral for Dad. We, the family, had not made our entrance yet, but Lindsey was there, and seated. She told me she heard it. That's the history I feel equipped to tell.

- You do not have to get every date and time perfectly.
- Most family history research is remembering.

MECHANICAL DAYS

YOU WILL NOT BE WRITING EVERY DAY. EXPECT MECHANI-
CAL DAYS. YOUR MIND WILL CONTINUE WORKING WHILE
YOUR HANDS ARE BUSY ELSEWHERE.

If you think spending a day on the floor surrounded by scrapbooks and diaries and high school yearbooks isn't working on your project, you are incorrect. If you think sitting outside in the sun, putting labels on your file folders, is a waste of time, you are incorrect again. These activities are important to the success of your project. So is taking a bath or a walk, or reading the newspaper. Every day something in that paper will remind you of something you want to write down. You'll tear it out, and stick it in the proper folder. Once you start working in earnest, everything you do adds another element.

We deserve mechanical days: copier day, or putting the notebook in order day, or filing day (copier day is best of all with its slow hypnotics). We need respite days for focus, and for cleaning off the desktop. Something new will always come to you. Your mind delivers to your door as reliably as Federal Express.

> - You are working on your project even on days you don't think you are.
> - The organizing elements of your work require time off from writing.
> - Enjoy these as effortlessly productive mechanical days.

ACCOMPLISHMENT DIARY

IF YOU SIMPLY WRITE DOWN WHAT YOU DID TODAY, AND AGAIN, TOMORROW, YOU ARE PROVIDING A GOOD LOOK AT THE SEGMENT OF LIFE KNOWN AS NOW.

When I first moved to California, I had never seen a mountain in person. Now the San Gabriel range was outside my window. The mountains felt huge and hulking to me, as if they blocked me away from anyone and anything I had ever known. I thought the only advantage to being so far away from home was that it was excellent practice for dying. Even the three-hour time difference served to alienate me. I may as well have moved to Mars, in my depressed opinion. I was the opposite of adventurous, filled instead with fear and loneliness, which translated to general gloom.

We had exotic flowers—too spiky for my liking, of course—growing all around the house. They were called birds of paradise. I felt even botany mocked me. I didn't know who I was or where. I felt erased.

One day I found a Japanese day book at the Friends of the Library book sale. It was a diary for 1974; this was in 1982. All the words were written in Japanese and all the pictures were of outer space and moons. There was nothing in the book that I could understand, and nothing that corresponded to anything familiar. It was a book after my own heart with lined pages on which to write. I chose this book to assure myself I existed.

I did not record feelings in this book. Instead, I wrote down each day's achievements.

- changed sheets
- planted ornamental corn
- went to grocery
- watched TV
- cleaned toilets
- did checkbook
- watched *Urban Cowboy*
- bought a skirt
- watered roses
- made hamburgers
- read *Esquire*
- ate sherbet
- mailed Mom coconut shampoo

- James Taylor on TV
- John Belushi died
- dreamt I knew Tom Petty
- animals to vet
- car wash
- read papers
- stayed in pajamas all day

I wrote in this diary every day. It has become one of my central possessions. It is a straightforward picture of a certain place and time. We all have days we can't define. These are messages to myself from when I lived in Japanese outer space.

> - Sometimes you say important things when you feel you have the least to say.
> - Minimal notes recall maximum memories.

CHAPTER FIVE

Collection

EVERYDAY ARCHIVES

YOU HAVE TO LOOK NO FARTHER THAN YOUR CLOSETS AND
CUPBOARDS FOR FAMILY STORIES.

Family history hides in plain sight. Just as our bones are library shelves, and our minds are filing systems and tape recorders, our homes and neighborhoods are research labs, think tanks in the creation of a personal history. An attentive drive through town reveals volumes, and cleaning out a closet is a course in anthropology.

Each room in your house is a country, unique with its own language. That country has a past stored in the cupboards and closets and in the pictures hanging on the wall. In your child's closet, you may find the nursery balloon lamp you couldn't give away, even when your child went to college. There may be toys you have not seen in a decade, but you could pick them out in a lineup. They are representative of your child's childhood. They are divine.

When you see sleeping bags, you hear sleepovers; when you see a vaporizer, you hear a nasty cough; when you—when I—see the beheaded Ken doll, I hear Karen laughing. Karen was my daughter's best friend in California. She lived just up the driveway. One look at beheaded Ken and I hear that wonderful, neighborhood Karen laugh.

Take a look around your own closet. The hats. The belts. The shoes put away in boxes. The shoe boxes filled with everything but shoes. Business cards from a town you used to live in. Dusty stamps and diaper pins. I love the sturdy wooden hangers proudly bearing logos from fifty years ago, when a department store was a department store and a hanger was a hanger. Nana kept a beautiful closet. I took the everyday archive hangers for my own when she died.

Our archives are all around us. Every item is a story. This becomes clear when you move. You put your hands on everything. You touch your life as it goes into boxes.

The things we use are the things we honor. Look through your toolbox. Where did you get that hammer? Look through your recipe box. How many people's handwriting do you find?

History is not all big event Saturday nights. History is an errand on Saturday morning. The things we touch are the things we treasure.

> • Our personal archives are all around us, in the
>   everyday objects we use.
> • Each object translates to another story.

PARTIAL JUNK GENEALOGY
RESOURCE LIST

I tend to practice the lazy man's brand of documenta-
tion. For years, I kept large, open-mouthed jars in logical
locations and dropped things in them as I happened by. I
did not think, "Here's a perfect icon of 1980." I just
dropped items in jars as I went about my business, and
when the jars were full, I'd start another.

I thought they'd be great to open up one rainy day,
maybe a day at the end of a bout with the flu. So I did. I
spread a throw blanket over the bedspread and spilled
out the contents of a jar.

I found a ringside ticket stub to the 1980 Tough Man
contest and a red and green calendar from Butch See, my
Columbus Dispatch carrier. There was a wire casing from a
champagne cork, a HELLO MY NAME IS badge, paper wrap-
ping from French lavender soap, a Friends of the Library
card, a plastic strawberry, plus a ticket to the Tracker
Band's private New Year's Eve party held at the Somewhere Else Bar and Lounge. A bathroom tile, a lock sawed
off a diary, a mood ring that is eternally a disconsolate

shade of black. Naked lady miniature playing cards, a rejection notice from an art show, a poker chip, a baby sock, the cow from the Christmas creche, and a ticket from Republic Airlines Flight 374 to LAX, where I have written: "I had dreams about a fire."

There was the condolence card from my friend Gliquor that came when my Grandma Ethel died. A tiny toy hanger and a newspaper photograph of a newspaper photographer. The phone message from the creep who called in the middle of the night to lie to us that he had found our lost dog at a false address.

There's a want ad that I answered for my first newspaper job. It says: WE'RE LOOKING FOR A FEW GOOD PENS. There's a note from Lindsey. "It's so weird," she wrote, "how our lives are filled with busy, everyday things." There's a crumpled four of hearts.

Here are some everyday items that hold memories:

- photo albums
- old sewing kits filled with knitting needles and embroidery supplies in tin boxes
- prescription bottles
- jewelry boxes

What jewelry do you wear? A wedding band? A pin of your mother's? A watch of your father's? A charm bracelet? Where did you get the charms?

Here's an idea that sounds goofy, but you might try it for fun. One day, put on a piece of jewelry that belonged to one of your relatives, something you don't usually wear. I chose my Grandma Ethel's charm bracelet with the names of all of her grandchildren engraved on individual gold disks.

It was inscribed beautifully with ornate, pride-in-workmanship script. I noticed that my disk was facing a different direction than all the other grandkids', and knew what must have happened. My dad never could remember how I spelled my name. (It's Debby with a Y!!! Dad! NOT I-E . . . Y!!!!!!!) He must have sent the bracelet back to the engraver to have my disk fixed, and the engraver, sick of the project already, attached it backward.

I wore this charm bracelet on my errands one day, just for fun. I put on a little lipstick, too. My hair was pulled up into what I like to call a boop. I got my love of hair ornaments from Grandma Ethel. To me, a drugstore hair ornament display is breakfast at Tiffany's.

Clerks were nice to me that day. Not that they usually aren't nice, but that day they were nicer than ever. I was nicer than ever back. Funny how that works.

Just by wearing her bracelet for a day, the essence of Grandma Ethel surrounded me. I was eighty-three and vibrant, a friendly woman going on her little missions, making them the high point of the day. Enjoying the moment, hair up in a plastic boop.

- Little Lane cedar chests
- collections you put away years ago, china dogs, dolls from foreign lands
- scrapbooks
- diaries
- pots and pans, egg poachers, mixing bowls, custard cups
- lists of books you've read
- baby books
- signatures in your high school yearbook

What are your personal staples? What stuff do you keep around the house all the time?

I save the items from my bulletin boards. I have photographed the inside of my cupboard and dishwasher. I have even photographed the contents of my refrigerator before and after a trip to the grocery store. I know I go overboard. However, I'm not sure our great-grandparents ever would have believed "I Can't Believe It's Not Butter."

- address books
- budget book
- phone bills

- answering machine tapes
- record albums, tape cassettes, CDs, whatever comes next
- sheet music
- quilts and blankets, electric or other
- button boxes
- holiday ornaments
- perennials in the garden
- snow shovels, leaf rakes, summer sprinkler attachments
- packed away sports equipment
- tools
- all those boxes of slides
- board games, Legos, half-filled sketchbooks
- aftershave and perfume bottles

Were your parents fancy dressers? When you think about them, what do you remember them wearing? Did your mother wear a fancy perfume? Did she keep it in pretty bottles on her dresser? Did your father wear cologne or aftershave?

Lindsey and I took a walk through our old neighborhood. She decided we needed a destination, so we walked to her mother's new apartment, the place where her mom moved after living fifty years in the same home.

The apartment is her mother's solitary dream palace, in a building housing many senior citizens. It feels both hometown and exotic with that certain worn leopardskin fabric chic only Happy (yes, this is my friend's mother's chosen name) can pull off.

Every surface is a memory. Each item she brought from the house was on the hit parade of Happy's "pretties."

"You're going to love this," Lindsey said to me. "This is my favorite favorite." There in Happy's bathroom, completely surrounding the sink, was blue bottle lined up next to blue bottle next to identical blue bottle. Maybe twenty of them in all, blue bottles in the curvaceous, womanly shape of Estée Lauder's Youth Dew.

"This is our life," Lindsey said, at the altar of the blue perfume bottle.

Decades of days diffused in a sweet-smelling mist.

- saved correspondence and back files
- awards, trophies, ribbons
- report cards, notes from teachers, paintings that hung on the refrigerator
- quotations that seemed important at one point
- samples and receipts from home repair projects
- the rag bag, table linens, bags of fabric scraps
- checkbook registers
- magazine clippings

Finally, I hope you save your calendars. Everything is there. The days of car pools and orthodontia, the days of babysitters and going over to play. Meetings of arts organizations and community groups. Days of ceremony.

Plumbers, wallpapers, and anniversaries. Scout troops, soccer games, your dinner with those people in Florida.

When Karen's brother died young, so young, I was able to look back at my calendar and count the number of days—eleven days—between the time my family moved next door and the time we became loving friends.

The New Year doesn't begin at midnight. It begins when you pull out your sharpest marker and transfer family birthdays onto your fresh calendar, the new one you've picked to carry you through all you're bound to encounter this year.

It becomes a holiday in and of itself, this day of transferring dates that are so personally indelible they ring chimes in your mind on their annual round.

These are the same dates you've been marking every year since your first calendar, the one you may have found in your Christmas stocking, along with a paddleball, a Golden Book, and a new box of crayons.

And ever since that first calendar, the one that originally made you feel that this next year belonged to you, you've taken out your best pen, your marker, or crayon and flipped through the pages and marked down the days that felt like no other: your mother's birthday. Your father's birthday. Your grandmother's birthday. Your grandfather's birthday, the days of your very creation. These are the days that link up with your own shining birthday to complete the circle that defines your life.

• Family history surrounds you.

CUSTOMARY SOURCES
MYRIAD RESOURCES EXIST TO HELP YOU TRACE YOUR FAMILY TREE.

You will probably want to utilize some of the more customary genealogy resources for the dates, places, and names that make up the specificities of your family tree. The Internet offers extensive research help: the Church of Jesus Christ of Latter-Day Saints, genealogy's geniuses, operates a website containing information about hundreds of millions of family names. Their Family History Library in Salt Lake City, Utah, is a researcher's paradise, and many cities across the country have LDS Family History Centers with helpful resource people who are happy to get you started, no matter your religion. Resources are available, too, for individual ethnicities. Those of Hispanic, Chinese, Jewish, African, and Native American heritage can find information in specialized libraries and websites.

Your local library is the best place to begin. You'll be searching for some of these documents: birth and death certificates, military records, and records of marriage and divorce. Land deeds and estate records are helpful, as are census records and city directories. Mortgages, naturalization records, tax records, wills, and phone books contain needed data and clues. Add atlases and maps, immigration information, parish registries, adoption papers and name changes, ship passenger lists, probate papers, and passports to your list of documents to seek. Don't forget the cemetery, and the family Bible.

Your family left footprints from the beginning. With diligence, you will be able to pick up the trail, and add some of your own.

• Check standard genealogy sources, along with your own files, for family facts.

CHAPTER SIX

Tips and Tricks

PRIOR NOTICE

I am going to suggest some tricks, tips, and pointers that are so elemental you might find yourself complaining, "She calls *this* a tip?" I am doing it for a personal reason. I like to know what to expect when at all possible, and I appreciate prior notice of any foreseeable bends in the road.

Here is how I got this way.

I started my job as a newspaper columnist never having been in a large daily metropolitan newsroom. I was clinically afraid of freeway driving, and would need to drive over an hour on two of Los Angeles's busiest if I wanted a new career. I had never used a computer. I was so green I glowed.

However, I got there and auditioned for three weeks. In order to get the job, I had to produce twelve acceptable columns written on a machine that worked against me—My father used to say, "A poor workman always blames his tools"—because of my lack of expertise. This was in a room full of hundreds of people who did not even have cubicles to separate them. They worked in "pods," heads down, necks horseshoe-shaped, at long adjoining tables. They played "The Flight of the Bumble-bee" in muffled computer-key clackety clack.

When someone sneezes, do you say, "Gesundheit" or "God bless you"? Do you have other sayings that just naturally come out of your mouth?

My boss-to-be was suffering from some horrible influenza, sneezing and hacking through my first day. The entire experience wrenched my insides. I was still trembling from the freeway and as germiphobic as Howard Hughes, saying, "Gesundheit" and "God bless you" and "Now, tell me again what happens when you push this key?"

The computer system was, for some reason, labeled in Olde English style. Instead of DELETE, its cross-out function button was marked RUB OUT. I asked my employer-to-be why this was, in my friendly, curious, journalistic fashion.

"I don't know. Achoo," she said. "It's British for eraser or something. It doesn't matter. It just is."

"OK," I said. "God bless you."

Three or four days into this situation, remember that I had three weeks to write twelve acceptable columns or it was back to the want ads for me, I told my boss I lost my column. I pressed a button and it went away.

She looked at my keyboard and at the offending button.

"Is it gone?" I said.

"It's gone," she said. "Achoo." She still had the flu.

"God bless you," I said. "What do I do?"

"Start over," she said.

"Start over?" Now I'm cold and clammy. I feel sicker than she does. "That's all I can do? Start over? Why did that key do that?"

"It just did. It doesn't matter. That's all you can do," she said. "But the good thing is, you'll never forget this. You'll never hit that key to save a piece again."

I never did. However, this is not the way I like to learn. I prefer to learn by hearing tips and tricks so obvious they make you say, "She calls *this* a tip?"

❄ *TIPS* ❄

NOT THE NEWSPAPER OF RECORD

My previous job had been at an alternative paper where we used heavy white electric typewriters with red dots on them. Their design reminded me of the Japanese flag. I never "composed" at the typewriter before this job, which goes to show, you learn when you have to.

We used the "X" key to mark out mistakes. All our stories looked cross-stitched together. It was a wonderful place to work with a small, funny, brilliant staff. Our most liberating statement was "We're not the newspaper of record." This did not mean we did not have to be accurate, it just meant we didn't need to be humorless and all-inclusive. If something was happening at city hall, we could choose to write about the quirkier aspects of the story. We could doodle on top of the straight lines constructed by the local daily. They were the announcers, we were the color people. We could concentrate on the nuts rather than the bolts.

You are not the newspaper of record, either. Someone has already written about the Great Depression, the labyrinthine medical system, and World War II. What your readers want to know, the story only you can tell them, is what those days were like for you, what you saw, and how you were affected.

Are you particularly careful with your money because of your family's experiences in the 1929 stock market crash? Do your children or your children's children agree with you about the value of a dollar? Do they think the way you do about long-distance telephone charges? Do they buy designer clothing when you think store brand would do?

Have you ever had to summon 911 in an emergency? What conversations have you overheard in your doctor's waiting room?

Do you have any military clothing stashed away? Is it your father's, your brother's, your sister's, or your own? What did you eat when you were in the service? When you get together with buddies to tell war stories, what stories do you tell?

Do not feel that you must recount the history of the world. If you put down your experiences, you are adding your individual insight. You are making history interesting and human.

My great-grandmother called her best friends "Mrs." The newspaper of record would not tell me that.

- Using every day detail as fact, you add a layer to the history of civilization.
- You are not the newspaper of record. It is not up to you to provide a vast overview.

KEEPING IT PRIVATE

You may not want to tell others that you are working on your project. It's a bit like telling people you are pregnant. For the next nine months all you ever hear from them is "When is the baby due?"

Preserving a family history can be a solitary process. You'll be going deep into your heart's hometown, looking at things you have had in storage there for years. This emotional process may not be something you want to casually mention in the grocery line or at a party. You may want to keep the exercise to yourself, like a hidden twenty-dollar bill in your pocket. How seldom it is, in this day and age, that we get to think about a thing and not discuss it.

You may want this to be the matinee you attend alone. You may not want to dissect the plot. You may just want to enjoy the show.

> • You may choose not to tell anyone what you are working on.

SUPPLIES

The office supply superstore was one of the more empowering turns retailing took in the twentieth century. Office supplies used to have a certain mystique; hanging files, boxes full of pens, manila folders—they were workplace-specific and said "working person" as loud and clear as a business card. They were coveted in a place of business, locked away and doled out like candy at Halloween. They were pilfered. Memos would circulate about them. You were afraid to invite work friends over for a bite to eat, thinking they might spy that ring-topped steno pad that snuck home in your briefcase or that lead-foot tape dispenser that must have stowed away on your commute.

*What was your first job? Your first real job? Did you start out in
an after-school job that had any relation to what you ended up
doing? Were you as nervous on the first day of your real job as
you were on the first day of your after-school job?*

I used to be a receptionist who ordered office supplies on
the side. This was my job description. I would tally up
roller ball pens by point thickness and color: black, blue,
red for the accounting department, green for seasonal
Yuletide cheer. Then there were the Flair pens for those
tasks that needed flair. Everyone had preferences. The
pen is as mighty as the sword and pen preference is as
personal as your favorite ice cream. Woe be to me if there
were only micropoints on hand if the boss wanted mini-
micros.

I ordered manila folders with tabs on the right side,
tabs in the middle, and tabs on the left side, plus hanging
files, both plain and box-bottomed. This was in those
dreary days when hanging files only came in govern-
ment-issue green. I spent hours perusing the office supply catalog. No one else was allowed to use it, lest they
notice a paper clip caddy in smoky gray that matched
their drawer divider so divinely that they just had to have
it, as if their desk had become a supermodel and these
smoked gray plastic items were the perfect pumps.

Don't get me started on the electric pencil sharp-
ener! I had to chain it down in the copy machine room
like a TV in a cheap motel. We had a standing appoint-

ment with our own office supply salesman, a guy by the name of Paul, and he would sit with me on the mauve velveteen lobby couches while an interim receptionist said, "Good morning, Ron Rees Company, Good morning, Ron Rees Company," in syncopated counterpoint to my carefully constructed order.

Item by item, I'd go down the list of Paul's delicious inventory. Two boxes number-ten heavyweight mailing envelopes. Seven six-roll packs three-inch adding machine tape. Five cartons white bond paper letter-size, four cartons legal.

It was a secret language, a parallel world of unthought-up-yet thoughts, and busyness of the future. The day the order would arrive was like Christmas. I'd crawl out of the supply room, hands cut and sticky from packing tape and corrugated cardboard. I felt both the pride of a shopkeeper with well-stocked shelves and the knowledge that a few days hence, I'd be a looted Mother Hubbard.

Office supplies—the employers' come-on. A fresh legal pad holds all the promise of a newly sharpened pencil. It's school supplies all over again, the fresh air of new beginnings.

I once worked in an office where they'd give you pens one by one. The maximum take was three at a time. This was a posted rule. You could go to the locked cabinet yourself, after acquiring both trust and the key from an apologetic administrative assistant. The key ring had a big plastic cookie on it—chocolate chip with a droll bite taken out. You would record your bounty in a special notebook, to be checked and counter-checked come judgment day.

D. G. Fulford. April 8. Three pens, one pad of paper.

- Some easily available supplies make your family history project go smoothly.
- File folders, small notepads, a looseleaf notebook, and three-hole paper are good to have on hand.

LITTLE NOTEPADS

Keep little notepads all around your house. Keep one on your nightstand, one in the kitchen, one beside the armchair where you sit in the evening. Keep one in the car. Either buy a contraption that suction-cups the pad to your windshield or put it on the passenger seat and don't allow anyone to sit there.

Keep one in your purse, plus one in your coat pocket. I like those that look like legal pads in Munchkinland. Capture words like butterflies whenever they come your way. Save them for your sentence collection.

A word leads to a sentence. A sentence leads to a paragraph. Have a notepad and pencil ready.

You drive by the schoolyard with your windows rolled down and you hear the children playing. Suddenly you can see the game of hopscotch you played with the girl across the street, and the yellow chalk she used to draw expert hopscotch boundaries. You remember the way the tether ball rope hurt when it wrapped around your arm and the bully who, one day and one day only, sweetly pushed you on the swing.

Not all writing is done at the keyboard. Memories happen when you aren't even thinking about your project. Catch them on notepads, which you have made available like little landing pads for floating thoughts.

• Keep notepads in convenient places. Pencils, too.

FILES

I advise people working on *To Our Children's Children* to get a stack of file folders and label each one with the chapter headings in the book: "Facts," "Family and Ancestry," "The House of Your Growing Up," and so on. Or label your file folders the way your own segments seem to be breaking down. This may not be apparent early on, but remember, you will need files. This is where all the notes from your little notepads go. When you harvest your notepads, you will find that your scribbled notes fit different categories. Tear them off and file accordingly.

When I had a garden, I would go out there every morning with a "What have you done for me lately" look on my face. Every day there was some small progression; growth happens invisibly and overnight. Notepads are your indoor garden. Pluck the fruit and put it in a folder. Newspaper clippings will follow, then old letters and photos and anything that reminds you of something else.

Keep your folders upright and easy to get at. Use a desktop stand or a rolling plastic milk crate.

When you are ready to write, take a folder to your desk and spill out what you collected. That clutter is the brilliance and epiphany you didn't let escape.

• A filing system is the best way to organize your notes.

ODE TO THE THREE-HOLE PUNCH

After I moved to Nevada, I worked six hours a week at what I refer to as my stapling job. This was at the Nevada Women's History Project, a repository for the biographies, autobiographies, and artifacts of some of the most individualistic women this country has known.

The state coordinator of the project was a woman named Jean. She was a legislator and activist who had been awarded one of the state's highest accolades: Distinguished Nevadan.

She was a completely competent person. I have never seen anyone so sure of how to get a project done. I, a lowly jester, who could not even photocopy addresses onto address labels so they would fit, often wondered why she hired me. I'm sure she did, too. I skipped a whole paragraph in the typing test at the job interview and never learned how to use her computer program; it was like electing a mime as Speaker of the House. So I was assigned other tasks. I was to staple and operate the three-hole punch.

Wondrous efforts took place in that office as we worked to recognize the lives lived by women in our state. We compiled a list of six hundred books in Nevada libraries and began to find out if women were included or omitted from these permanent accounts.

This project was done by volunteers. They chose books to read from the list, then carefully reviewed them on lengthy questionnaires printed on different colors of paper. Each color signified a separate genre; biography, fiction, poetry, reference, community, or regional history. My job was to punch three holes into those questionnaires and place them in a notebook.

I loved this job, a simple yet integral task. The course of history looked at in human terms moving at a human pace. People power, Jean liked to call it.

Folders were labeled in freehand script. The point was to get the job done, not to dillydally about it or label with a label-making program. This was a space of pens-without-caps, used vinyl notebooks, and donated desks existing on borrowed time in the downtown YWCA.

The important job of preserving honest history was done right here, led by one of the most capable, driven women in Nevada. It was done in the simplest of fashions, exemplifying the short form. Collection, consolidation, execution using tools a jester mime monkey like me could use.

Let this be my ode to the three-hole punch, and a guarantee that your family history can be done with an absence of bells and whistles. I wish Walt Whitman could hear America singing on the loose-leaf notebook aisle.

- You do not need fancy equipment to do your family history project.

FIRST DRAFT

A first draft means your words don't have to be well chosen right out of the gate. Pieces can be added and deleted, and paragraphs can be switched around. The first draft is the foundation, the skeleton, the bones. It has constructed itself from the piles of paper you've been writing and consolidating. The piles that grew from the single sheets you dared to begin. The first draft includes what's scribbled between the lines.

· · ·

If you're anything like I am, you'll be a wee bit crazy until that foundational skeleton forms from the capricious shapes of your memories, wondering if it will ever come together or doubting the wisdom of your decision to do the work at all.

The best news about the first draft is that the second draft has no blank pages.

When the bones appear, you'll pick up momentum. You'll flesh out sections, adding muscle and heart. Then you'll hear the heartbeat as your stories start coming to life. It will sound familiar. It belongs to you.

- The first draft is the foundation you build upon to tell your story.
- No more blank pages.

WEEK OFF

If I were a university professor, I would be known as D. G. Gut Course because I profess it is always a good idea to take a few weeks off.

The prerequisite for taking this time off is doing your work and letting the pages stack up. Keep writing, keep adding pages, but do not read them. Build your stack like a cord of wood. When an idea comes to you for a change or addition, just scribble it on the page with one hand covering your eyes. Consider rereading to be peeking.

One day, take your pile of papers outside or upstairs, to a different space from your usual place of working. Bring a pencil with you. Be a baby and count the pages. It is a preliminary way of gauging where you might be, even though you'll only be done when you're done. Call it temporary satisfaction. For the time being, it will do.

Then read your writing. Don't be critical or cruel, just read it. See what needs to be added and what could be taken out. Mark places where you feel you have repeated yourself. Shingle the pages with Post-it notes with arrows and ideas on them.

Don't rewrite. Don't labor to reconstruct sentences. Just mark the places you'll need to come back to. When you come back. After your week.

This is a big project you've taken on. Don't belittle that fact. You could use a vacation.

Check your progress, see what direction you seem to be taking, notice which questions interested you most, what subjects you enjoyed writing about, as well as the subjects you didn't. Then plant daffodil bulbs, go up to the lake, or finally get your hair done. Take those books back to the library. Check out more books and read them.

When the odd sentence or thought about your family history project pops up, write it down on your notepad, knowing you will get back to it later. After some time off, you'll see things differently and catch a second wind through an open window. You'll go back reoxidized and ready. Gut Course class dismissed.

- Don't belittle the size of the project you've taken on.
- Take time off. Prepare for this by marking pages with ideas for changes. This way, when you get back to your project, you'll know where you can easily start back up again.

SWEET INSPIRATION

Don't forget to be inspired by others. This project has you deep inside yourself, your head swimming with words and people. Come up for air, looking and listening for wisdom, wherever it may be.

Who is your favorite artist? Have you ever seen his or her work "in person" or only in books? Do you know much about the artist's personal life? Do you identify with the artist's life in any way?

My favorite artist is Pierre Bonnard, unless you count Saul Steinberg. I love Bonnard for what he said, as much as I love him for his paintings of the bathtub, my favorite place. Bonnard said he wanted his paintings to show what one sees when one enters a room all of a sudden.

. . .

Your family history project has you putting on new eyes to enter your old rooms. Sometimes those eyes get weary. Let a genius pep them up. Read, listen to, or look at the work of someone you admire; you can't always be your own inspiration.

Tape great quotes and picture postcards all over your work space. Some days I fill my head so full of aphorisms there could be a revival meeting going on in there.

Here are some words that have helped me over the molehills through the years. Some of the quotes are attributable, the sources of others disappeared long ago when I first tore out the phrasing that brought a smile to my eyes.

"Without vision, a line is simply straight."

"And the thing is, if you got it, you always got it, you know?"
— JOHNNY CASH

"Take a pie home to someone nice."
— MARIE CALLANDER

"My body never prospered when I was writing. It just puts a state of tension and stress through all your system."

"Keep yourself to yourself."
— STEVE EARLE

"As this movement entirely absorbs my time, I hardly leave the house."
—MOHANDAS K. GANDHI

But when I do leave the house, I love to walk through a plant nursery or a fabric store, the library. Nothing takes you away like going to the movies. I also prescribe nights of TV and slick magazines for myself. I zone out. My most loved book for creative inspiration is *The Art Spirit* by Robert Henri. I read it when my daughter was a toddler and I was a toddling adult, wondering what we were both going to grow up to be.

> • Get inspired by others' work.

THE WHOLE SHEBANG OF IT

What's your favorite saying? Can you remember where you first heard it?

Beginning your story is difficult, so start in the middle. The beginning has a lot of responsibility. It is a pre-summing up, attempting to introduce the whole shebang of it. (This is a phrase I heard from a New Yorker and have loved ever since.) It's hard to know what the whole shebang of it is until you're at the end of your writing project.

In English class, they used to talk about the denouement. This is the outcome in a story where all complications are resolved, and mysteries and secrets are explained. This sounds very nice, but we're not writing fiction.

We are writing about our lives, and lives don't seem to have denouements. My friend Carol believes that the first moment of the afterlife is a denouement. Think of that. All your big questions answered.

The first question in *To Our Children's Children* is a little question.

What is your name?

This is a get-your-feet-wet question. You don't need to start there. You can start anywhere you want. You can start in the middle.

Begin by writing about your neighbors, and the last book you read. About your Tuesday afternoon bridge game, or poker Wednesday night. Start wherever you feel like starting. Start even though you're not sure where you're going. You will get to the beginning by the end.

• It is acceptable to start in the middle.

PICK A CARD, ANY CARD

When you don't know where to start, start like this: Open *To Our Children's Children* to any page, run your finger down the list of questions there, and choose the one your finger lands on as the story you will tell that day. Yes, Virginia, there are times we feel we're wearing donkey ears instead of party hats. If we do this, though, the pick a card, any card method of writing, we've turned an effort into a magic trick.

This private parlor game is not all silly. It removes the heavy mantle of "family historian" and brings back the quality of light this project deserves.

I once read that Andy Warhol used to eat a can of Campbell's soup for lunch every day of the week. Day in, day out, Campbell's soup. A harbinger of art to come? Could be, or perhaps it was financial necessity in his starving artist segment. Naturally, he worked his menu inertia with a twist. He would remove the labels from all the cans, so whichever soup he chose that day would be a surprise. He'd pick a can, any unlabeled can, open it up, and eat it. Mystery took precedence over craving for alphabet or beef noodle.

I love this story because it illustrates how simply we can add a moment of harmless lottery to our day. It's going to the mailbox, always expecting something wonderful to arrive. What am I going to write about today? OK. Page 121, question 18.

What's your perfect lunch? What's your regular lunch?

I have no idea if Andy was ever so disappointed with his pick that he fed it to the dog and chose another. I don't know if he held himself to some moral code that made him eat the soup he picked, to dance with the one that brung him.

I do know that if you are not in the mood to answer the question your finger pointed out, close the book, open it again, and choose another. If you don't like the coconut haystack, maybe the next one will be a caramel. If you don't like the caramel, maybe the next will be butter cream.

I can't let this Andy Warhol story go by without discussing my favorite question in *To Our Children's Children*. I get asked this a lot, and always come back to this one.

What is your favorite Campbell's soup?

I love this question because it is self-effacing and boundless. Soup bubbles on the back burner of our collective psyche. I've heard wonderful answers to this question— utterly different stories—and each makes absolute sense.

One young reporter at a large metropolitan newspaper said that her favorite soup was . . . I forget. See, it's not really the soup; it's the story. But let's say her favorite soup was tomato. This reporter said that years ago, when she was a little girl, she had a working mother. Working

mothers were fairly rare in her community, but her
mother's job gave this child, this woman reporter, something she didn't realize until she sat down and thought a
moment about Campbell's soup.

She made dinner for herself some nights as a little
girl. She remembered that, on those evenings, she would
usually make soup. She'd open the can by herself, heat
the soup by herself, pour it into her own bowl and eat it.
Years later, the reporter saw soup as a source of the inde-
pendence that made her proud as a girl, and prepared to
do whatever was called for as a woman.

Another reporter remembered lobster bisque as his
favorite soup (though it wasn't Campbell's lobster
bisque). He remembered lobster bisque that he ate his
first time at the Atlantic shore. He was on vacation with
another family and they had all been to this shoreline
before. He had not. He felt out of place and homesick.
Then someone in the family handed him this pink-
orange soup. Suddenly he had shared experience; he felt
welcomed. A simple question about Campbell's soup
sent him on a meaningful vacation again.

An older woman read the question and recalled a
time that she, like Andy Warhol, ate Campbell's soup
every meal of every day. She moved to Manhattan
straight out of college, having no idea how expensive it
would be to live there. She needed to save her money for
a winter coat and Campbell's soup was her savings plan.

A mother sent her son off to college with the requisite lessons on laundry and cleaning and cooking. But he phoned home with an urgent question. He'd been to supermarket after supermarket and nowhere could he find the Mason brand soup his mom served at home. Of course he couldn't. She put it up herself, in Mason jars.

- Pick any question to work on. If you don't like that one, pick again.
- Not every question needs to be answered, and they needn't be answered in any certain order.
- Your answer maybe something only partially related to the question. That's fine. A memory is a memory, a story is a story.

THIRD PERSON

If somewhere in your heart you think writing about yourself is braggadocio and puffery, self-importance and sinful pride—all the Me, Myself, and I of it—try writing in the third person.

For example: He quit college to work and help out his family. He fell in love, got married, and went off to war. She was a dance instructor who always took jobs at the schools where her children would get the best education. From elementary school through college, they have been able to drop off their books in her office and visit during the day.

Think of these as blurbs in *TV Guide*, describing this week's episode: "Marcia falls in love with the island while on vacation and decides she never wants to leave."

It feels funny to put down a version of your life in an "as told by" fashion. But it's another way of looking, more new eyes.

• As an exercise, try writing about yourself in the third person.

TEN MINUTE LIMIT

Set a time limit and make it short. Tell yourself you have fifteen minutes, or only ten. Make these the minutes right before you need to get dressed, start fixing dinner, or before your favorite show begins. Choose the time precisely to rush yourself, even though you're already so rushed you have no idea how you're going to do this project at all.

When you know you're going to work for a minimal amount of time and not one minute longer, it is not as difficult to sit down and do it. Once you've sat down and done it, you'll have done it for the day. You can watch reruns guilt-free and have a starting place when you revisit your work. This takes the pressure off. How perfect do you have to be in ten minutes?

Brief is better than nothing, and often better than long. This hurried remembrance might contain the living breath missing from other stories you've struggled with. You felt free, not all hunched over like a human question mark.

Time limits can go either way. Sometimes you need uninterrupted blocks, other times you only need ten minutes. You will find yourself working with both because of the way life is and what the day brings. Consider it cross-training. Aerobics one day, yoga the next.

> • Set a ten minute time limit some days.

PACE

Work at your own pace. Otherwise, you won't do it. Don't let your eyes turn to cartoon pinwheels. Take a walk, do an errand, go outside. Don't push yourself. If your mind is not there today, you're excused. If you have planned to work for an hour and a half and are spent after an hour, fine. Get up. Put your papers in a pile. Tomorrow is another day. They will be there when you return.

Don't overdo it in one sitting. Moderation in everything, even family history. Go get a glass of water and stare out into space. Close your eyes awhile.

We are self-propelled machines, and what works for one may not work for another. Some people are raring to go in the morning, while others can't begin to think about their project until they're finished with the matters of the day.

We are hard on ourselves about so many things: We're too fat, we don't follow current events closely enough, our paint is peeling, and so forth. If we have embarked on the trail of family history, then we deserve a pat on the back, a kiss on the cheek and John Glenn to wish us Godspeed.

- You must work at your own pace.
- Everyone has a different concentration span.
- Take breaks.

ARBITRARY DEADLINE

I did not mean to demean the deadline in all of that talk about personal pace. A deadline is one of the most helpful tools a writer has, despite its morbid name. You cannot work on a newspaper without coming up against a deadline. We are not working for newspapers, though. We are working for ourselves and for our children's children. Set your own soft deadline, arbitrary and flexible.

Be doubly sure to allow yourself plenty of time to enjoy your project. You will have days off, you will get colds, you will need built-in time to let your mind meander.

There are glorious side trips in your family history project, little bed-and-breakfasts of discovery along the way. You can spend three days looking over an old scrapbook. You can unearth a box of photos and compare your great-grandmother's profile to your profile, viewing ancestry in a backward mirror.

The books you see in a bookstore usually took a year to write and then a year to publish, so don't rush with yours. You've sped through enough of life. Why not take your time remembering?

If you want to present your family with your finished project for a holiday, anniversary, or birthday, start early and don't panic. Traveling the scenic, circuitous route takes time, but it's an interesting ride.

Did you ever sleep in a train's sleeper car? When was your first time on an airplane?

Looking through some of my dad's papers, I ran across his father's life insurance policy. My grandfather took out this policy in May of 1918.

Question 1 G on the application form asked: Have you ever taken an aeroplane flight? (Give details). My grandpa answered, No.

Question 1 H on the application form asked: Do you contemplate doing so? No, my grandpa answered.

I applied for health insurance in 1999. The application form asked me if I ever partook in skydiving, and did I contemplate doing so. I answered, No.

I don't think being a daredevil runs in our family.

> • If you are planning to have your project finished by a certain date, be sure that deadline is far enough in advance to allow for off days and digressions.

CHAPTER SEVEN

Side Effects and By-products

UNEXPECTED BENEFITS
WRITING CLEARS YOUR HEAD.

Writing your family history is not a completely altruistic project. Of course, the intended result of your work is a keepsake for generations to come. Yet you will be a different person for having done it, for paying real attention to your life and accomplishments, for looking again at the hard times and good times and seeing how far you've come.

Recent studies suggest writing is therapeutic. I think of it as demagnetizing your brain. If your brain were, in fact, a tape recorder or VCR, it would tend to get gunked up with all those family stories and memories swirling around in there.

Putting your stories on paper serves the same purpose as a tapehead cleaner. It clears your head and allows you to organize the mishmosh. You'll see patterns and progress, and that's only the beginning.

You can carry what you've learned out into the community. You can interview others, help them tell their stories. *To Our Children's Children* has been used in writing groups for senior citizens and school classrooms, in local oral history projects, historical societies and museums, even hospice settings.

Personal history is a focused look at life. What is unique is also universal. You'll encounter side effects and benefits you may never have considered.

• Carry *To Our Children's Children* out into the
  community.

INTERVIEWING OTHERS
PEOPLE LIKE TO BE LISTENED TO, NOT JUST HEARD.

Even though they might protest, throw the same excuses at you that you've thrown at yourself ("My stories aren't interesting." "Who would care?" "My memory isn't what it used to be."), when push comes to shove—when talk comes to listen—you are doing a service by lending an ear.

You may want to interview family members for your project, or you may take your skills into the community, urging others to tell their stories. Oral histories are as important as taxes in civic preservation. Interview alumnae of the local school system or members of a Rotary Club. Get the folks in a garden group to speak about the specifics of growing roses in your region. Ask church groups questions about the changes they've seen. Talk to people who dance or make ceramics. Talk to elders and youngsters. Motivate them to interview each other. The only prerequisites are evocative questions, sincere curiosity, and an open mind.

Oh yes, and a working tape recorder. Make sure your mechanics are in place. Check your batteries and cords, and label your tapes as soon as you are finished. Be aware that it is less confusing to interview one person at a time than the entire garden group at once.

You can feel an interview take flight. The interviewee may start out reticent, but something will get him or her going. Nothing draws a person out more easily than knowing someone cares. If your subject gets off the track, remember that the track is never perfectly straight and that one story leads to another. If the stories get confused or repetitive, gently introduce another question about a different subject.

Have people spell proper names if they can. Ask them to explain any acronyms. For instance, JPL means Jet Propulsion Lab.

I know a woman who recorded her elderly mother and began to get frustrated at the toll the years had taken on her mother's mind. But she kept at it and she got answers. It was amazing, this woman told me. My mother couldn't remember what she had eaten for breakfast that morning, but she could tell me the name of the pony she and her sisters rode to school seventy years ago.

Have compassion and patience. Whatever you get is golden. And turn off the tape recorder should you be asked to do so.

"My husband's name was Edward, but everyone called him Funny," a woman told me during a community-based oral history project.

"Funny?" I laughed. "That's funny! Why did they call him Funny?"

"Because he was funny," she said, and she began to cry. We turned the tape recorder off and sat still a moment. At the end of the tape, she can be heard singing a song and reciting a poem she'd written.

- Oral histories are invaluable in civic preservation.
- Be sincere and compassionate.
- Make sure your tools are in working order: fresh batteries, proper cords, and outlets.
- It is preferable to interview one person at a time.
- Label your tapes.
- Remember, have all audiotapes transcribed.

COMMUNITY

YOUR HISTORY RELATES TO YOUR NEIGHBORS' HISTORY.

Our stories link up with others' stories like charms on a charm bracelet; individually beautiful, yet maybe more lovely combined.

My mother's cousin Lois—Mink's granddaughter—shared her written history with me. My mother and her cousin are both eighty years of age. They grew up in the same town and have lived just blocks from each other all their lives. My mother's cousin and her husband were my parents' closest friends; best men and maids of honor in each others' weddings. In our town, their names are as synchronous as love and marriage, as horse and carriage, as peanut butter and jelly. Phyllis and Bob. Lois and Harry. Macaroni and cheese.

I remember my mother and her cousin pregnant with younger siblings. I remember them dressed up for parties and laughing on the porch, in shorts. I have seen them smoke cigarettes and not smoke cigarettes. I have seen them in bright swimsuit coverups and dressed in deep charcoal and black.

I have watched them at forty, fifty, sixty, seventy, now eighty. Never had I—never could I have—seen them as four-year-old girls.

*Did you have any friends who went with you all the way from
elementary school through high school?*

Until I read Lois's history. She wrote about the two of
them attending Miss Fanning's Nursery School. Two tiny,
little things, wearing tiny, little dresses. I hold this unseen
image in my mind, and can pull it out like a picture of my
daughter from my wallet. Eighty-year-old women. Four-
year-old girls. Walking beside each other for a lifetime.

Our individual stories can't help but intersect with the
stories of the people who have been most important in
our lives. When a group shares memories, it is possible to
recreate a community on paper that does not exist anymore.

Do you have a porch or a balcony where you sit?
What did he say when he asked you to marry him?
What did she answer? Where were you?

Recently I had the opportunity to visit the house where
Lois lived when she was a girl. It was all fixed up for a
charitable event. Interior decorators had redone every
room. More than fifty years before, my father and
mother announced their engagement at a big party
there. They shared their happiness from a balcony off
the master bedroom.

I had to go see for myself just how *Evita* this was.

I'd been to these designer showcase houses before, so I knew to expect the velvet cords roping off rooms, as in a museum. What I had not anticipated was the docents' talks about Lois's family, the original owners. They spoke about them in such bygone terms they sounded like milkmaids and bootblacks you'd see on a visit to Williamsburg.

I had just been with Lois, watching CNN! It was disconcerting. Relatives turning into ancestors in twenty-four hours' time.

> *What did the house of your growing up look like?*
> *Was it stone or wood? One story or two?*
> *Was the house you raised your family in*
> *big enough for all of you?*
> *If you decided to move from the family home,*
> *what was the deciding factor?*

Just a few days before I had been looking—just looking—at "empty nest" housing for my mother who lived twenty-six years in one house with my dad and almost twenty years in another. Before that, there had been apartments, Army housing, and her parents' house.

That was the house she wrote about when she wrote about her father.

Which was around the corner from Lois's house. Where they practically played the minuet when it became a designer showcase in 1999.

When our stories connect with others' stories, they become outdated maps of the community, invaluable archives.

Most maps show streets and parks and rivers. Few show sidewalks where tiny girls in tiny dresses walked together to school.

• Your story is both individual and communal. It paints a picture of another time.

GROUPS
STRENGTH IN NUMBERS.

Many people find it beneficial to work on their family history venture in a group setting. Think of it as a book group where books are written instead of read.

One person's memory will jump-start another's. "Hey," the formerly forgetful might think, "something similar happened to me."

To Our Children's Children has been taught around many tables. People of all ages and backgrounds gather together and share. The commitment to assemble once a week or twice a month provides continuity and camaraderie, something sitting alone lacks. Some use a group as an additive to their solitary project. Gathering can grease all those gears and wheels in one's head.

Stories beget stories. We learn about ourselves, we learn about each other.

Los Angeles defines multicultural living. So many people from so many places speaking so many languages in so many accents. So many traditions. So many customs. So many stories. So much to learn.

I worked with one writing group consisting of a woman from the East Coast who grew up in a wealthy family as well as a man who spent his youth on a Nebraska farm. There was a Japanese lady and a Latina, also a Caucasian woman married to a man from the Middle East. There was a married couple, native Hawaiians, and a woman from the Bronx.

They told simple stories; this and that. The man from Nebraska talked about his farm.

"It was perfect," he told us. "It looked just like things are supposed to look but never do."

The lady from the East Coast said she was glad to hear the stories. Her life had taken her from one coast to the other and she had missed, she said, all the fine colors in between.

We talked about fences, hedgerows, boundaries. About laundry lines and talking to your neighbor.

What was the big business in the town you grew up in?

"Our grandchild went to school and told her class that her grandparents were slaves," said the woman from Hawaii. The grandmother always wondered about that, and then the explanation dawned on her.

"We had told her we lived on a plantation. A sugar plantation! That's why she thought that!" she said.

We saw each other differently at the end of every session. Each person opened up their drapes and gave the rest a peek inside.

No one can remain a stranger who is willing to share that way. No one can remain an enemy if you know what her favorite bedtime story was or how homesick he got when he went away to camp.

Use the buddy system to motivate yourself. Join or form a writing group. If you think there's strength in numbers, imagine all the strength there is in words.

- A family history writing group is one interesting way to work on your project. Spend some of your class time writing and some reading assignments you've worked on at home.

REUNIONS
GET THE WHOLE FAMILY INVOLVED IN THE PROJECT.

Remember tricky Tom Sawyer and his entrepreneurial savvy in recruiting others to help him in the interminable chore of whitewashing the fence? You can do the same thing in putting together your family history. An upcoming family reunion or a holiday like Thanksgiving is the perfect place to start.

As we now know, a family history needn't be a straight-ahead narrative. It can be a collection of stories. A combination of parts creating a whole.

Stories can be gathered from far and wide, from aunts and uncles and distant cousins. If you are planning a family reunion, send each member a different question from *To Our Children's Children*. Ask them to send their answers to you (or your more organized sister) in time to assemble the stories into book form. It will be a party favor they'll never lose.

Did your family ever have a reunion? Did you meet any relatives there you had heard a lot about but didn't know?

Or try this. Have them bring their answers and read them aloud. What better way to get to know one another? Put the questions in a bowl and have relatives pick them out at random. Stick a question underneath each dinner plate. Tape-record and transcribe the answers. Have each family bring a box of photographs and point out who's who.

The informal method is wonderful. Zero tolerance for fret. The project is no less viable just because it's fun.

I met a man in Reno who organized family reunions every five years. These were educational as well as social. Each branch of the family was assigned a book to read— meaningful, important books. Part of the reunion time was dedicated to structured sessions. Relatives reported on what they had learned and how these lessons could affect the family in a positive way as it moved forward.

Get your family members talking to one another; sharing, discovering, and learning. A reunion is a bringing together. Share yourself with the people who share ancestry with you.

- Share the work.
- Send *To Our Children's Children* questions to family members prior to a reunion. Assemble their answers into a book.
- Ask and answer questions extemporaneously.
- Assign each branch of the family a chapter, or allow them to choose their favorite. Have them "report" the stories they recall to the others.

CHAPTER EIGHT

Frequently Asked Questions

NUNYA
BUT WHAT ABOUT THE BAD STUFF?

I get asked a lot about the bad stuff. Everybody has bad stuff. Does it belong in a family history?

If you want it to, it does. If you don't, don't put it in. There is no law of full disclosure here. This is family history, not a confessional. If it helps you to write about it, write about it. If you don't want anyone to read it, crumple it up and toss it away.

Shred it.

This is not lying by omission. This is protecting your zone of privacy. You are not paparazzi assaulting yourself. You are taking a look at your life and your times. If you want to edit, edit. You have creative control.

Writing helps, though. You gain a page worth of perspective. When you find yourself in an emotional jungle, writing helps you scythe your way through.

What were the hardest times in your marriage? Was there ever a time when you felt it might really be over?

Ours was the most civilized of divorces. I pulled my files labeled BANK JUNK and TAX JUNK and hauled them over to his house. I am not a numbers whiz, so he was going to crunch them, or do whatever one does with numbers to appease the IRS.

We watched TV when I got there. I think there was a basketball game on. Then he said, "Deege, we need to get going on this deal."

He meant the divorce, not the taxes. He was tiring of our limbolike, separated status. He said he felt neither here nor there.

I said I felt fine. I'd been cruising. I'd been on a hiatus of the heart and was feeling comparatively happy with the elements in my life.

His lawyer, though, had a tickler file and sent him periodic reminders.

I could not help but picture a greeting card showing a basset hound in a funny hat, saying, "Whoops! Isn't there something you've forgotten to do?"

Oh yes, that pesky divorce.

"It will be like *Terms of Endearment,*" I told him. "The part when Emma dies and Aurora says, 'I thought it would be a relief. It's not a relief.' "

We had been living separately for three years, but the cord had not been cut. Lawyers were going to cut it and I pictured him on the home ship, safe and secure, and me tumbling through space, an astronaut adrift forever.

"Now don't go getting funky," he said.

I got funky. I cranked the radio and made an obscene gesture at his office building as I drove past. It was wimpy anger, anger I didn't even feel. It was anger in anticipation of hurt, anger facing fear, anger reluctantly passing denial.

I left BANK JUNK and TAX JUNK at his house and knew the day I picked them up would feel different from the day I dropped them there. And I took solace in the fact that everyone in the country hates April 15, too.

No one leaves this life unscathed. We goof up. We shame ourselves. Untoward tragedy happens. We can't pretend life passed by with no potholes or sinkholes. In my family we have a saying, though. My brother Tim thought it up: Nunya.

As in, Nunya business.

Not every story is for public consumption. You don't get points for pulling skeletons out of the closet and rattling them in your unsuspecting loved ones' faces.

To play the Nunya's advocate, though, there are positive aspects to the negative. Sometimes you do a service by not painting your life in a greeting card glow.

The whole point of your life is to learn. If you learned something that might help a family member during difficult times, it doesn't hurt to pass it along.

Were you ever fired or laid off? How did you cope with that? Did you define yourself by your job? Has retirement been a positive or negative experience?

You quit your day job. You're a no-collar worker.

You're on retreat, you have not retreated. You are accepting uncertainty. You are in the wild blue yonder. You are getting down to brass tacks. You are living sensibly as the best revenge. You are fiddling while Rome burns.

You are divining. You are playing it by ear, following your nose, trying to watch your back. You are Marcel Marceau walking against the wind.

You are whittling to the bone, you are throttling back, you are going toward your essence. You are doing what is essential. You are facing the inevitable. You are not backing down.

You are improvising. You are redecorating the room for improvement. You're in no-wheel drive, headed to the devil's workshop. You are penciling in, you are crossing out. You are revising. You are reconstructing.

You are off on a tangent, getting your bearings, putting one foot in front of the other. You are praying to God and rowing to shore. You are an escapee. Papillon. You're waiting for Godot, or somebody like him.

You are transitioning. You are seeking terra firma. You are wearing your tabula rasa on your sleeve. You are changing shape. Transmogrifying.

You are a Saturday morning cartoon show and it's intermission. There's been an interruption. You are adjusting. You are altering and permutating. You are innovating and transitory.

You are emancipated. You are free at last. You are exploring the options of your own volition.

You are released under your own recognizance. You left your Rolodex in your other pants.

You are on the leeway. You're on the Leeway Freeway.

You are seeking your own level.

You are progressing. You have great expectations. You are on your way to the verge. You are turning the page.

You are exceeding your metes and bounds.

On our way driving from California to Nevada, my daughter amused herself by asking me some of the things I'd recently learned that I never knew before.

Like pumping my own gas for the first time on my forty-eighth birthday.

And learning one must pull over when driving slowly on mountain roads, so faster motorists can pass.

And then we hit a deer.

Sometimes you can make a slight change of words that invites a change in thinking. To look at more than just the sting. Not to dwell. Just to look.

I saw an obituary for a baby. Instead of "stillborn," this family wrote "born silently."

Our children get something from understanding that things were not always perfect for us. Things are not all going to be perfect for them. It might help them if we told them how we managed to get through.

Choose to include your sorry moments or choose not to. Label the file NUNYA. This is your book of memories. That doesn't mean it has to include every single one.

How do you keep from crying when you cut onions?

I don't. I see it as a perfect opportunity to go ahead and cry.

- A family history is not a confessional. Writing about the hard parts helps, but you do not have to include what you would rather not include.

LENGTH

HOW LONG SHOULD MY FAMILY HISTORY BE?

I have heard from some people who answered every question in *To Our Children's Children*. Most people pick and choose, as if the book were a menu. One woman wrote to say she has written family histories at three different stages of her life, each time from a different perspective.

One of the most heartening I've read is Tommie Lancaster's of Grandview, Missouri. One page. Black ballpoint pen on yellow legal paper. Mr. Lancaster wrote:

I was born in Cleburn County, Arkansas, in a sawmill camp. I am 94 years of age, and in good health. We will have been married 65 years on the 15th of June. We reared three children. Put all three through college, all married to college graduates. All have good jobs and good homes. All have two children in each family. We have one great granddaughter. I had two careers, 21 years in military service, 22 years a cabinet maker.

I thank God for all the guidance I have had and blessings I have received. I never could have reached this point without supreme guidance and help. I had a sixth-grade education. My father was killed in a sawmill explosion when I was 9 years of age. I had one brother and one sister younger and one sister and one brother older. We lost our mother when I was seventeen. Now I am the sole survivor of my family.

Ninety-four years on one piece of paper; a satisfied summary of a difficult life lived well, with faith and determination. A one-page story like this would thrill any family.

You will know when you are finished with your story. It can be a page or it can be volumes.

If you are like Tommie Lancaster, it can be volumes on a page.

• Only you can decide the right length for your family history. Some do it in a page, some a volume. Some pick up the writing habit and continue on.

DO IT NOW
WHEN IS IT TOO LATE?

Never. When my dad was in his bed, near death, my daughter came to visit one last time. He wasn't eating— nothing tasted good to him. His mouth was dry and his lips were cracking.

My daughter thought of sweet Italian ice and went to two stores before she found some. She brought it home, and fed it to her grandfather with a spoon. It was cherry.

"Italian ice," my father said, and began reminiscing. He had been stationed in Italy during the war. Pretty soon he was telling a story, using all the dramatic flair he ever had. He was an entertainer again.

He talked about a village and he became each villager, with his voice alone. He used an Italian accent, all lilt, melody, and expression. My mother, my daughter, and I were transfixed, bursting with delight, tears, and admiration, listening to a living, loving libretto from a dying man.

It was as if Botticelli's angels were singing to one another, flying around my parents' bedroom.

Opera from Italian ice. A memory.

Bellissimo.

PRESENTATION
WHAT'S THE BEST WAY TO PRESENT A FAMILY HISTORY?
WHAT'S IT SUPPOSED TO LOOK LIKE WHEN IT'S FINISHED?

It may be in book form, it may remain a three-ring notebook. It may be in a bound journal, it may be duplicated at the copy shop or on your computer. The methods of reproducing the written word and restoring photographs are easier and more attainable now than ever.

However, the speed of technology leaves obsolescence in its wake. Are video cameras the stereopticons of the twenty-first century? Natural disintegration of materials and normal life attrition can cause problems. Check with those knowledgeable about archives in your area. There are sunshine concerns and dust concerns and moisture concerns and storage concerns and a whole other set of concerns about textiles. Look in the Yellow Pages or on the Internet for supplies and expert opinions. Ask a librarian for answers.

How to organize those words? Use the chapter headings in *To Our Children's Children* and whatever segments they lead to. Or divide your account by decades. Some people decide to put their memories together as a cookbook of favorite family recipes.

Cook together. Someone cooks, someone writes or records.

A number of people keep track of time by lists of books they read. I did. Naturally, I didn't date it, being a longtime student of the nineteen-whatever school.

Some knit family trees on sweaters. Remember Happy and her perfume bottles? When she was nineteen she typed a booklet of all her favorite poems; the ones that taught her something about love, life, death, honesty, bravery, judgment, humor, and acceptance, as she wrote then. She saved her pages and at seventy-three, made forty copies to give her loved ones.

Some family histories are leather bound; some are Post-its on a journal page held together by a rubber band.

The way you tell your story is your own; by chapters, by hobbies, by decades, with photographs, by sinks, by typewriters, however the piles fit. What it looks like, in the end, will be as varied as the stories. The presentation—the gift—is up to you.

It is you.

- There are as many presentation methods as there are stories.
- Reproduction of words and photographs is easily attainable.
- Be sure to use archival supplies.

CHAPTER NINE

Fruition

INVISIBLE THREAD

So here we are at the end.

What have you done? What do you have?

You have something to hold in your hands, then pass along to future generations. Something that adds words and color and life to the names on your family tree.

You have collected, composed, and come to fruition; creating genealogy, a loving reference book.

You looked at life segment by segment, under a microscope. You recorded your findings. It was not unalloyed bliss.

You did not set out to tell the story of civilization, but you did that too, somehow.

*Who delivered to your house? A milkman? A laundry man?
An egg man?*

Who would you add now? The pizza guy? The hospice angels? UPS?

History is not only big things. History is little things. What we call our best friends and who delivers to the house. Those are the pieces you've stitched together into your nonlinear line.

Your lineage.

My nephew has a distinctive walk. He walks with his arms held out a little, away from his sides. His grandfather walks the same way, his mother's father. My nephew did not grow up in the same town as his grandfather. He has seen his grandfather walk, of course, but not so early and repeatedly that this would be imitation or imprinting.

This is more than that, and more than DNA.

This is the unseeable made seen, in our children and our children's children. The connecting line that defines the constellation of family. Consistency, Continuity, Continuation.

SEVENTH SINK

I remember my life in typewriters and I remember my life in sinks. It was at this sink, my seventh if you'll recall, that I felt the invisible thread move through me.

What is your specialty food item you prepare for a gathering,
potluck or party?

I was making deviled eggs for our first Fourth of July without Dad. We never considered that the Fourth of July
would be a hard holiday. When the World War II veterans
came down the parade route, though, my mom finally
burst into tears. Then I did, then my aunt Sue, then my
cousin Molly. We recovered. We went swimming in the
pool, but there was a Dad-sized hole. He very wasn't there.

However, that morning, during deviled egg prepara-
tion, he was. In the way I cracked open the hard-boiled
eggs. There was my dad and I couldn't shake him.

Not that I would have wanted to shake him. You know
that by now.

The thing is, I saw so clearly that he could never leave
me, that some of him was contained within me. From
hard-boiled eggs, of all things.

It was the way I roll an eggshell across the counter to
crack it. That's how I watched him do it and that's the
way I do it, and on the Fourth of July, I understood how I
would always have my dad.

By thinking about him, and knowing his habits. By
recognizing one in me when I found myself at it. Cracking eggshells, looking out the kitchen window, standing
in front of my seventh sink, before the parade began
down Roosevelt Avenue back in my hometown.

Denouement.

ENDISPIECE

Can you think of one memorable thing that each one of your children said, something that surprised you or amused you or impressed you at the time and still sticks in your mind?

When I first started to write, I didn't realize I was writing. I was typing, a sentence here, a sentence there, song lyrics mostly that were running through my mind as I prepared to move to California, where I didn't want to go.

I started typing these "typings," as I called them—never realizing what they would lead to, therefore feeling no anxiety about them. Messing around trying to fix the typewriter allowed me to escape. Instead of packing, I'd worry with the ribbon. Instead of dealing with real estate agents and mortgage papers, I'd brush the keys with oil, trying to get them to unstick.

"And then there was the change" is the first sentence in my typings. And then there was the change, in fact. I moved, I typed, I kept on typing. From repetitive radio lyrics to vicious complaints and secret hopes, from descriptions and disappointments to things that struck me funny, my typings kept me going, one sentence—one memory, now—at a time.

. . .

Then one day my nine-year-old daughter said to me, "Mom? You know what I'm going to do when you die?"

I said, "No."

"I'm going to go get your typings, take them to my house, staple them all together, and have a good laugh," my daughter said.

This was fifteen years ago and it is still the best reason I can think of to keep typing. To keep writing it down.

To contact To Our Children's Children, please write:

> To Our Children's Children
> 6956 E. Broad Street
> Suite 245
> Columbus, Ohio 43213

On the Web, access *www.familyhistories.com*

Thank you.

ABOUT THE AUTHOR

D. G. FULFORD is an award-winning writer, a nationally bestselling author, instructor, speaker, and former columnist of the *Daily News* of Los Angeles and *New York Times* News Service. Her first book, *To Our Children's Children: Preserving Family Histories for Generations to Come,* written with her brother, syndicated columnist Bob Greene, has been America's number-one-selling guide to writing family histories for several consecutive years.